Incredible Vegetables
FROM
Self-Watering Containers

Incredible Vegetables

FROM

Self-Watering Containers

EDWARD C. SMITH

Storey Publishing

*The mission of Storey Publishing is to serve our customers
by publishing practical information that encourages personal independence
in harmony with the environment.*

Edited by Gwen Steege and Carleen Madigan Perkins

Art direction by Cynthia McFarland

Cover design by Kent Lew

Text design and production by Jessica Armstrong

*Front cover portrait of author by Sylvia Ferry Smith;
back cover container shots © Giles Prett/Fotografix*

Interior photography credits appear on page 244

*Illustrations by Brigita Fuhrmann: 108 bottom, 110 top,
111; Kurt Musfeldt: 105, 106, 107, 108 top, 109, 110
bottom; © Elayne Sears: 14, 20, 24, 32*

*Indexed by Christine R. Lindemer,
Boston Road Communications*

The information in this book is true and complete to the best of our knowledge. All recommendations are made without guarantee on the part of the author or Storey Publishing. The author and publisher disclaim any liability in connection with the use of this information. For additional information please contact Storey Publishing, 210 MASS MoCA Way, North Adams, MA 01247.

Storey books are available for special premium and promotional uses and for customized editions. or further information, please call 1-800-793-9396.

Printed in the United States by R.R. Donnelley
10 9 8 7 6 5 4 3 2 1

LIBRARY OF CONGRESS CATALOGING-IN-PUBLICATION DATA

Smith, Edward C. (Edward Clarke), 1941-
  Incredible vegetables from self-watering containers / by Edward C. Smith.
    p. cm.
  Includes index.
  ISBN 13: 978-1-58017-556-2; ISBN 10: 1-58017-556-2 (pbk. : alk. paper) - ISBN 13: 978- 1-58017-557-9;
  ISBN 10: 1-58017-557-0 (hardcover : alk. paper) 1. Container gardening. 2. Vegetable gardening. I. Title.
  SB418.S63 2005
  635.9'86--dc22
                                                                                2005033224

DEDICATION

SYLVIA FERRY SMITH — *gardener, photographer, my best friend, and my wife — is co-creator of this book. Sylvia and I developed the ideas of this book together, and we planned, planted, and tended the gardens where this book grew. Sylvia both made the garden photogenic and took many of the images. This book would not have been possible without her.*

CONTENTS

PART ONE
Get Growing
in Containers

CHAPTER ONE

A NEW WAY TO GROW VEGETABLES

Almost all the vegetable gardeners I know grow food for their families in the good soil of their backyards. But what if you don't have a backyard? How can you keep the kitchen stocked with ripe tomatoes or fresh greens if all you've got is a patio, deck, or balcony?

Potting It Up

What about a garden of containers? Gardeners have, after all, been growing flowers, herbs, and ornamental plants that way for ages. If you can grow pansies or petunias in a pot, why not peppers, peas, or pak choi?

Well, it turns out you *can* grow peppers in a pot (or peas, or pak choi, or even eggplant, lettuce, or spinach). Vegetables will grow in the same kind of container and by using the same methods that work for flowers and other ornamental plants. Just take a traditional pot (something with a hole in it to let excess water drain out) and fill it with potting soil, fertilizer, and a plant. Add water, and then add water again whenever the soil dries out. The plant will grow and produce food.

In some ways, gardening in containers is easier than gardening in the earth — the garden plots are small and simple to manage, plants are less likely to be bothered by diseases or pests, and there are almost no weeds. That's the good news.

But it's not all good news. I discovered three things that bothered me about growing vegetables in containers the way gardeners have traditionally grown flowers in containers. One has to do with watering; one has to with results; and one has to do with the way the plants are usually grown. The solutions I found to the following three problems form the core of this book.

Problem #1 Compared to an earth garden, a traditional container garden requires you to lug out the watering can or hose at least once daily, and often more than once a day. Because vegetables tend to be large plants that grow quickly, they need a lot of water and they need it all the time. The constant watering also creates another problem: all that water coursing through the container takes with it some of the water-soluble nutrients in the soil. As a result, the traditional container gardener needs to add fertilizer regularly.

Problem #2 Even when they are watered regularly, most of the vegetables we grow in an earth garden don't grow as well in containers; sometimes the difference between a vegetable grown in an earth garden and one grown in a container is striking. It is possible, if you're willing and able to spend a lot of time watering, to grow a pepper or a tomato in a pot. But if you use a traditional container, neither the pepper nor the tomato will grow as well or produce as much in a container as it would in the earth garden.

Problem #3 Finally, the methods traditionally used for growing edibles in pots are not organic. In my earth garden, I use organic methods. I'd like to do the same in my container garden.

◀ *Gimme water. Even demanding plants like this artichoke thrive in self-watering containers.*

A Self-Watering Solution

One solution to the problem of constant watering is the self-watering container. A self-watering container is different from a traditional container in that it doesn't have a hole in the bottom. Instead, it has a reservoir for water and a way of making that water available to plants on demand. As long as there is water in the reservoir, soil in a self-watering container will not dry out. It seemed to me that such containers might make watering easier and less frequent, so my wife, Sylvia, and I tried growing some vegetables in self-watering containers rather than in traditional flowerpots. What began as a small experiment quickly became an entire garden of containers. Over the past three years, we have trialed more than 200 self-watering containers, growing almost everything we grow in our earth garden.

The self-watering containers did simplify watering. You do still have to water, but nowhere near as often. But that wasn't all that happened. I discovered that solving Problem #1 had inadvertently solved Problem #2 — almost every vegetable I trialed grew better in self-watering containers than it had in traditional containers. Many actually grew better in self-watering containers than they did in the earth garden. Tomatoes and peppers grow well in our earth garden, but they grow even better in self-watering containers, especially in years when we have too little rain. Eggplants and artichokes are a challenge for us in the earth garden even in the best of growing years, but they produce consistently good crops in our container garden.

▶ *Eggscellent! Most vegetables I've tried have grown better in self-watering containers than in traditional containers. Many, like this eggplant, actually grew better in self-watering containers than they did in our earth garden.*

▲ *Exit strategy.* As water leaves a plant through the foliage, it creates a pull that draws more water (and water-soluble nutrients) up through the roots.

TRANSPIRATION: the evaporation of water from the surface of leaves and stems.

Why Water?

The results of my self-watering-container trials strongly suggested that a consistent supply of water had something to do with the differences in growth between plants grown in the earth garden and those grown in self-watering containers. I realized that although I knew that plants need water, I was not really clear about *why* plants need water. I was, therefore, not really sure how much water plants need and how often they need it.

Why, then, do plants need water?

PLANTS ARE MOSTLY WATER

Like other living things, plants are made up almost totally of water, at least 80 to 90 percent. Water provides the firmness we observe in healthy plant tissue. Conversely, the sign that a plant has too little water is wilting: drooping leaves and stems. Plants that are starved for water produce fewer, smaller, and less juicy and tasty fruits.

PLANTS NEED WATER FOR PHOTOSYNTHESIS

Hydrogen, one of the basic plant nutrients, comes from the H in H_2O. During photosynthesis, photons (energy from the sun) break apart water molecules, freeing hydrogen atoms. The hydrogen then combines with carbon (from carbon dioxide in the air) to form carbohydrates — the building blocks of plant tissue.

PLANT NUTRIENTS PASS THROUGH WATER

There must be a film of water around each root hair in order for nutrients to pass from the soil to the plant. Whenever there is not enough water around the roots of a plant, nutrients fail to move into the plant, and growth slows. If the soil dries even more, root hairs dry out and die. At this point, the plant is severely stressed and growth is interrupted. Even if the plant survives the ordeal, the quality, size, and taste of the harvest have been compromised, and that plant is not likely to become the plant it could have been.

ALL CREATURES LIVING IN SOIL NEED WATER

In my experience, plants grow best in a soil that is alive, literally, teeming with mostly microscopic creatures that supply plants with food, creatures that help them to assimilate food, creatures that help protect plants from predation and disease. Those soil-dwelling creatures all need water. In the absence of water, they go dormant or die.

PLANTS NEED WATER FOR TRANSPIRATION

All of those reasons put together amount to only two percent of the water a plant needs. The other 98 percent of the water a plant needs passes through the plant and exits through its leaves by a process called transpiration. What a waste! Except, of course, that nature doesn't really waste anything; the water used in transpiration is essential to the normal growth and health of the plant.

Water leaving a plant through transpiration doesn't just leave; it creates by its leaving a force called transpirational pull, which both draws more water into the plant through its roots and provides for water movement within plant tissues. Plants don't have a heart the

▲ *Green is good.* The broad, flat leaves of broccoli catch more rays than the narrow, strappy foliage of other plants.

PHOTOSYNTHESIS: the process by which a plant uses energy from the sun (*photo*) to create (*synthesize*) carbohydrates from carbon dioxide and water.

way humans and other animals do. Transpiration is the plant's substitute for a heart; it is the way a plant moves fluids within itself. Without transpiration, plants could not move water and nutrients from the soil, could not make sugars through the miracle of photosynthesis, could not move those sugars about and change them into starches — could not, in short, grow, mature, fruit, and produce seeds.

Transpiration serves another important function — it dissipates heat from the sun (much like perspiration does in an animal). That cooling is critical to a plant's survival.

Consistency Is Key

Plants like the ones we usually grow in the vegetable garden need to grow large, and they need to do it fast. To do that, they require lots and lots of water. The bigger the plant and the faster it has to grow, the more water it requires.

How much water are we talking about? Not much research has been done, but we do know, for instance, that a mature tomato plant needs at least a gallon a day. I've noticed that a summer squash plant needs about the same. It is theoretically possible, by using continuous-flow watering systems with emitters, to meet the water needs of plants in traditional containers. But it is not easy. Different sorts of plants need different amounts of water, and the same plant has different water needs at different stages of growth. Water needs vary with air temperature and humidity. This is too much of a problem for me to take on if there is an easier way. Self-watering containers are that easier way. As long as there is water in a container's reservoir, a plant will always have as much water as it needs.

Continuous-flow watering systems also do not address the problem of nutrient loss. When water flows through a traditional container (in the top and out the hole in the bottom), it takes nutrients from the soil with it. This means that over the course of a growing season, you'll have to replace these lost nutrients by fertilizing. For plants that don't require a lot of nutrients — herbs, for instance — this may be a livable situation. For those that grow fast and produce heavily, the lack of nutrients will cause slower growth and lower yields at harvesttime. Growing plants like these in self-watering containers will require less fertilizing (and sometimes none at all!); since water is being taken *up* from the bottom, you can be sure that nutrients aren't being washed away.

◄ *Water well and be fruitful. Vegetables such as eggplants, peppers, and tomatoes need a consistent supply of water to reach their full potential.*

Organic Is the Difference

Problem #1 and Problem #2 can both be solved by the sort of container I choose to garden in. Problem #3 — how to garden organically and sustainably in containers — is solved by what kind of soil mix I choose to put in the pots. Because I believe that the health and productivity of a plant is dependent on a healthy and viable soil community, my goal in composing a container mix is not to feed the plant, but rather to feed the soil — which will, in turn, feed the plant.

As a result, our container garden is as different from traditional container gardens as our earth garden is from traditional gardens. Our plants grow healthy and strong, reducing the problem of pests and the need for pesticides. Because they get their nutrients from the soil and not from us, they do not depend on constant fertilizing to grow to their full potential. Most important, our plants are unbelievably productive (with much less help from us) and the food they produce is both nutritious and tasty.

Unfortunately, no other book on growing vegetables in containers will tell you how to do it organically. But it is possible, and I will show you how. Whether planted in self-watering containers or traditional pots, all of the vegetables, herbs, fruits, and flowers I'll tell you about in this book are grown organically.

▼ *Onions, anyone? Because of their shallow roots, onions thrive in self-watering containers, where they don't have to compete for water and nutrients. My organic container mix also ensures a bumper crop every year.*

CHAPTER TWO

A POT FOR EVERY PLANT

Gardeners have grown plants in containers for a long time. Some ornamental plants and many herbs are fairly easy to grow in almost any sort of pot. Vegetable plants, however, are not as easy to grow well in containers; to be healthy and fruitful, they generally need more water than a traditional pot can supply. Pairing the right pot with the right plant is the first step toward productive container gardening.

Traditional Containers

A traditional container is something — anything — that can hold some soil and has a drainage hole or holes in the bottom. The hole ensures that the soil in the container does not become waterlogged. Some plants can grow well in waterlogged soil (soil that contains water but little air), but most can't, including all the ones we want to grow in the vegetable garden. Edibles and many other garden plants need a balanced ration of both water and air; the hole in the bottom of a traditional container gives excess water a way to escape and helps maintain the balance of water and air.

Water begins to dribble out the hole in the bottom of a traditional container when the container soil is holding all the water it can. From that moment until the next time I water the container, the soil has progressively less and less than the maximum amount of water it can hold. Thus, there is less and less water available to the plant or plants living in that soil. This fluctuation in available water is one reason most vegetables don't grow as well in traditional containers as they do in earth gardens and in self-watering containers. That doesn't mean you can't grow edibles in traditional containers. But it does mean that, with a few exceptions we'll discuss below, you'll work harder for a smaller reward.

Some Like It Dry

All the vegetables we have tried grow better in self-watering containers than they do in traditional containers; vegetables need more water than they can get in a traditional container, and they don't like the cycle of wet to dry and back again that characterizes life in a traditional container. But if you're willing to put up with more-frequent watering and a smaller harvest, you can grow some vegetables in flowerpots. As a general rule, the smaller the plant, the less watering and fertilizing it will need.

Some herbs appear to grow just as well in either kind of container, though there are many that truly prefer the freely draining soil a traditional container offers. Also, I am told (by people with a more sensi-

◀ *From the top. Traditional containers are watered from above, until the soil is saturated and water begins to run out the bottom. This drainage is key to maintaining a balance of water and air in the soil, but also causes a loss of water-soluble nutrients.*

tive palate than I have) that herbs grown in a somewhat stressful environment taste better than those that have been living, as it were, on Easy Street. Apparently, herbs react to stress by producing more of the aromatic oils that make them what cooks want them to be. It may, therefore, be a better idea not to grow herbs in a self-watering container, because they won't suffer water stress and therefore won't be as tasty. (Perhaps there's a moral there — suffering creates character.)

For a few herbs, though, traditional flowerpots are the only way to go. Dill and cilantro will lose their leaves and then rot in self-watering containers. The herbs that shrivel and die in a self-watering container seem to share at least two qualities: their leaves are small, elongated, and fairly sparse, and they originate in a climate where they are used to a wet–dry cycle.

Most edible flowers grow well in either container, but gem marigolds suffer root rot from too much water when grown in self-watering containers. Nasturtiums grow far too well in self-watering containers; they turn into garden gorillas that grow wherever they please, thank you very much. I choose to grow my nasturtiums in traditional containers just to make them behave.

A Question of Size

Unlike the self-watering containers we'll discuss later in this chapter, traditional containers have no place to store water except in the soil with which they are filled. Because the *soil* is the water reservoir in this sort of container, more soil (and therefore, a larger container) is needed than would be the case if there was another place to store water.

▶ *It's a rough life. Most herbs don't like to live on Easy Street. They grow better and are more flavorful when planted in traditional pots, where they can dry out a bit. Almost anything, including a tea kettle, can be made into a planter. Just drill a few holes in the bottom for drainage.*

▲ *Pick your pot. There is an amazing array of traditional pots and cachepots available, many of which can be converted into self-watering containers.*

Store-Bought Pots

Traditional pots have been around for a long time, and virtually any garden center or hardware store will have a good selection of sizes, shapes, and colors. When I was growing up, hole-in-the-bottom pots were all made of clay, usually unglazed terra-cotta but also glazed, sometimes with pretty designs. We called them flowerpots, and we grew flowers in them.

Nowadays, traditional pots come in nontraditional materials — plastic and fiberglass, even metal. These materials are generally more lightweight than clay and are therefore a good choice for large pots. Because none of the plants I grow in traditional pots is very big, I don't have any need for pots larger than eight inches in diameter. A clay pot that size isn't very heavy, so I go the old-time route and opt for clay.

If I were growing anything other than herbs, flowers, and an occasional small vegetable plant in traditional containers, I'd be using larger pots. And because big clay pots are both heavy and fragile, I would choose some nontraditional, lighter-weight material.

Self-Watering Containers

A self-watering container, stripped to its essentials, includes a place for soil, a place for water, a way to keep the soil and water apart, and a way bring the soil and water together. When it's filled with a good container mix (we'll talk about what makes a good mix in the next chapter) and with some water in the reservoir, a self-watering container creates a growing environment that is ideal for almost all the vegetable plants we would consider growing in an earth garden. The soil in this sort of container is consistently moist but never waterlogged. Roots grow throughout the moist soil, even to just below the soil surface; all the plant-growth processes that require water proceed uninterrupted: nutrients pass from the soil to the roots and translocate to other parts of the plant; hydrogen from water molecules is always available for photosynthesis; the carbohydrates created through photosynthesis move from leaves to other places within the plant. And all of the soil-dwelling creatures that need water have it. Vegetable plants grow steadily, as quickly as they can, and the result is tender, tasty, and nutritious food for the table.

Self-watering containers are a relatively new development in the gardening world; they've been available only for a few years. New designs pop up yearly, and more and more catalogs and garden centers offer them for sale. Self-watering containers can be bought; other sorts of containers can be made to be self-watering. If you're crafty enough, you could even make your own self-watering containers from scratch.

HOW LONG WILL THE WATER LAST?

How long the water in your reservoir lasts will depend on many different factors: how mature the plants are (and thus, how much water they need to maintain growth); whether the plants are growing in full sun or part shade; and how high the temperature climbs.

Considering the worst-case scenario — a mature plant like this tomato growing in full sun during the hottest part of summer — it's reasonable to expect the plant to use up to a gallon of water a day. That means a self-watering container with a 16-quart reservoir will have to be refilled every four days.

The Anatomy of a Self-Watering Container

The reservoir of a self-watering container should hold enough water to meet the needs of mature plants for at least a couple of days. For large plants, this means a couple of gallons. Water gets into the reservoir through either a tube or a hole in the container side (the latter also serves as an overflow hole, to keep the soil from becoming waterlogged). A false bottom holds the soil away from the water and allows air to reach the soil from underneath. Most of the false bottoms have narrow slots so that air can pass through but soil can't.

Some sort of wicking system takes water from the reservoir and moves it to the soil. In some containers, the wick is a piece of capillary matting, analogous to the wick in a kerosene lamp. In others, some of the soil comes into contact with the water and serves as a wick; the water then moves by capillary action up through the soil. Some containers use both approaches. In my experience, they all work equally well. There doesn't appear to be any reason to choose one or another container based on the kind of wicking system it uses.

There will also be a way to measure the amount of water in the reservoir. This may be a float in the fill tube, an overflow hole, or a fill hole. Whatever method your container employs, check the level regularly.

▶ *Bottom watering. Self-watering containers draw water up from below, which avoids the loss of nutrients traditional pots experience. The reservoir also supplies plants with consistent moisture; as long as the reservoir is kept full, the plants will have as much water as they need.*

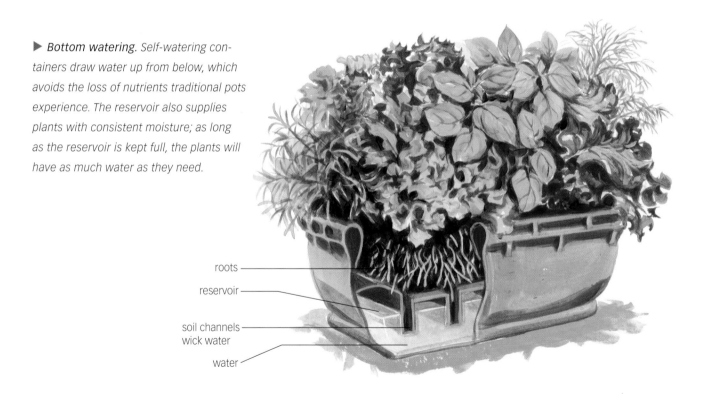

roots

reservoir

soil channels
wick water

water

Which Pot to Pick?

The amount of soil in a container — and, to a certain extent, its depth — determines what sorts of plants will grow well there. That's how we'll group containers for further examination.

A BIG FOOTPRINT
WITH MODERATE SOIL DEPTH

Large containers hold between 40 and 50 quarts of soil and as much as 16 quarts of water (enough to survive a long weekend without any damage to their contents, even when the plants are large and the weather is hot). That makes for a heavy container — as much as 60 pounds when full. I don't recommend moving full containers often, but if you must, make sure you've got help. If you anticipate needing to move containers a lot during the growing season, choose a style that has wheels or put the containers on a wheeled dolly before you fill them with soil and water.

AS WIDE AS IT IS SHORT

Deeper soil and a square or round footprint make a good home for root vegetables like carrots, beets, radishes, and turnips. They hold up to 50 quarts of soil and as much as 10 quarts of water (though the whiskey barrel holds a whopping 32 quarts of water!). In addition to growing root vegetables, they're good for single plants like eggplants, summer squash, mini pumpkins, and compact winter squash. With a trellis, you can easily grow peas, cucumbers, or a single tomato plant. Space other plants as recommended in part 3.

▲ *A garden of containers. Left to right: spinach, lettuce, summer squash, zucchini with lettuce, tomatoes with lettuce, and kohlrabi.*

BEST OF THE BUNCH

I have trialed many different kinds of vegetables in large self-watering containers, and the following have grown best for me:

- basil (12 plants)
- broccoli (2 plants)
- Brussels sprouts (2 plants)
- bush beans (18 plants)
- cabbage (2 plants)
- cauliflower (2 plants)
- chard (8 plants)
- eggplant (2 plants)
- lettuces (12 plants)
- onions (12–18 plants)
- pak choi (6 plants)
- peppers (2 plants)
- tomatoes (1 or 2 plants)

MOSQUITOES AND SLUGS, OH MY!

Inside the reservoir of a self-watering container is a dark, dank, moist space — the perfect habitat for some garden pests. The refill hole on a self-watering container can be an entryway for mosquitoes, which may breed in the standing water inside. That hasn't happened to me, but it has happened to other gardeners I've heard from.

I *have* had slugs enter the container through this hole, however. Some manufacturers now offer an accessory cover for the refill hole; I just plug mine with a piece of a copper scouring pad.

HANGING POTS AND WINDOW BOXES

A small step down, from large to medium, yields a container that is small enough to be portable but big enough for even a tomato plant, summer squash, peppers, eggplant, or celery. The reservoirs in these containers are not as large, however — they hold up to four quarts, which means that mature tomatoes or squash will need to be watered daily. In hot weather, I check the water level twice a day.

Hanging containers use space I'd otherwise waste. Besides, there's something alluring about the whole idea of growing vegetables in the air. I feel more intimate with plants I can visit at eye level, and I like doing some of my gardening standing up. These planters are only barely self-watering; the reservoirs hold just a quart of water. Plan on daily watering for greens or a small chili pepper plant. There's enough space here for half a dozen small lettuce plants, one chili pepper, or half a dozen herbs.

Window boxes are my favorite way to grow salad greens. They're easy to pick from, and the smaller sizes are portable enough to come inside for the winter and perch near a sunny window. For a real show, try growing some of the many colorful varieties of greens. The containers I have tried range in size from 23 inches (holding 17 quarts of soil and 4 quarts of water) to 39 inches long (holding 28 quarts of soil and 9 quarts of water).

▶ *Pots on parade. Self-watering containers come in all shapes and sizes. Clockwise from top left: A hanging pot of herbs is easy to water and to harvest from. Window boxes are an ideal way to grow lettuce. Even with just a small amount of space and a trellis, you can grow a bounty of tomatoes, lettuce, and nasturtiums. This large planter is practically the size of a small earth garden plot. A strawberry pot can be used for strawberries, of course, or for a variety of herbs.*

With this ready-made insert, you can turn your favorite pot or cachepot into a self-watering container in just a few easy steps. Whichever pot you choose, it should be between 16 and 20 inches in diameter.

WHAT YOU'LL NEED

- drill
- cachepot
- ready-made insert
- marker
- scissors

1 Drill a hole into the bottom of the cachepot. This will act as an overflow hole for times when your reservoir fills beyond capacity.

2 Drill a hole into each of the legs of the insert. The holes allow water to come into direct contact with the container mix.

3 Attach the insert to its reservoir.

4 Gently push the insert down into the cachepot and attach the fill tube. Insert the white water-level gauge into the fill tube.

5 Fill container with potting mix, pressing some mix down into the legs of the insert. Mark the water level gauge to show the reservoir depth and cut it off so the fill tube cover will close.

I think the pocket planter was originally designed as a strawberry garden; at any rate, it works for that purpose. If I had only one of these planters, though, I would grow herbs, rather than strawberries, in it. The herbs thrive. And it looks so good!

How often you'll need to refill the four-quart reservoir depends on what you're growing and how big it is; check the water level regularly until you've figured out the water-use pattern for the plants you're growing. Strawberry plants seem to be thirstier than most of the herbs. There are eight planting pockets, plus the larger space at the top, which can hold either a larger plant or more than one plant.

A CACHEPOT OR NOT?

Most self-watering containers were designed as such right from the get-go. They are one unit, with the self-watering components integrated into a plastic pot structure. If you're looking for a particular color or style, your options will be somewhat limited.

You can, however, create your own self-watering container with a cachepot — a pot that looks to be a traditional container but lacks a hole in the bottom, and is meant to be a disguise or a cache (hiding place) for a container that needs some dressing up. Cachepots come in innumerable materials, colors, styles, and sizes. Some cachepots can be modified to become either traditional or self-watering containers (see "Making a Simple Self-Watering Container," opposite), but unmodified they are not meant for growing plants. Soil in a cachepot will become waterlogged, and the plants in it will perish.

If you plan to make a cachepot into a self-watering container, be sure before you start that it is possible to make holes in the material. Some materials are difficult to make holes in, and others may shatter or break when you try.

▲ *Flowery snacks. An edible bouquet of pink dianthus, blue bachelor's buttons, yellow calendulas, and miniature sunflowers grows from a self-watering cachepot.*

CHAPTER THREE

WHAT'S IN THE POT?

What does it take to make a mix that is a good home for plants? Organic gardeners believe (as do I) that the secret is in the soil — that the millions of microscopic organisms living in healthy soil contribute to the health of the plants. The potting mix we will create for our containers, self-watering or not, will be a compost-based mix that's teeming with life.

Holey Soil!

To begin with, our mix needs to be full of holes. About 50 percent of a fertile soil, whether it's in an earth garden or in a container garden, isn't soil at all; it's pores — the spaces between soil particles, which allow air and water to enter the soil and flow freely through it. This is important for several reasons.

Roots need to be able to grow easily. If the soil is compacted (doesn't have enough air pockets in it), a plant will grow fewer roots and as a result will take up less water and fewer nutrients than it would if it had a larger system of roots. The result is a plant that grows smaller and produces less.

An organic soil is alive, and the creatures living in it need air to survive. When the soil becomes water-logged, the creatures that are beneficial for the growth of vegetable plants begin to die.

Plants can't take up nutrients without air. Plants need air around their roots for nutrients to pass from the water in the soil to their roots.

Thus, although we tend to think of soil as if it was just particles of matter, it is really a combination of matter and the spaces between matter. Some of the spaces, called micropores, are relatively small; they contain mostly water. The rest, called macropores, are larger and contain mostly air. In a fertile soil, water fills about the half the pore spaces and air fills the rest.

That's my goal — a soil that's full of holes. How do I get there?

▼ *Air it out*. A mix with good structure will have lots of holes, including macropores (large pockets of air) and micropores (small pockets of water).

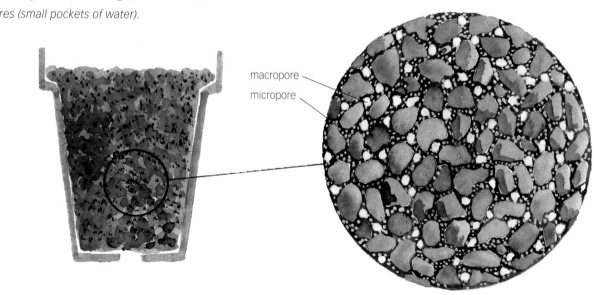

macropore

micropore

What's in Your Mix?

Whether or not your goal is to garden organically, the mix you fill your container with needs to be able to retain and move both water and air. The mix you'll be looking for is what I'd call a container mix or container soil, but that's not necessarily what the vendor will call it. It might be labeled *potting mix, potting soil, starting mix, transplanting mix,* or, sometimes, just plain *mix*. I'm not really interested in what the mix is called or even what the label says it's good for; I want to know what's *in* it. Knowing that, I can decide whether it's likely to be a good mix for my container garden. Most premixed potting soils contain some combination of the following:

Sphagnum peat. Partially decomposed remains of centuries-old sphagnum moss. The basic ingredient for many transplanting mixes, usually harvested from ancient bogs in Canada, it holds both water and air. It is organic matter, but it decays very slowly and adds little in the way of nutrition. It is very acidic, with a pH of 3.5–4.5.

Sedge peat. The ancient, partially decomposed remains of sedge, reeds, and grasses. It is of a darker color than sphagnum peat and holds more water.

Coco peat, or coir. Recycled coconut husks, used for aeration and water retention as an ecologically sound alternative to sphagnum peat, which is a very slowly renewing resource. It holds more water than sphagnum peat and has a pH range of 5.7–6.8. It comes in compressed bricks that must be soaked in warm water.

Bark and/or sawdust. Used as a basic ingredient in some potting mixes. It provides organic matter, but few nutrients.

MIXING FOR HOLEY SOIL

In typical container growing mixes, structure is created by combining two basic components: something that will absorb water and something that water will flow around. Although many different ingredients can be used to create this structure, a combination of sphagnum peat moss and perlite is the most common, and is also the best choice for self-watering containers.

▲ *The good stuff. High-quality potting mix like this one will have lots of visible perlite.*

WHERE'S THE DIRT?

Why not just fill your containers with topsoil from your earth garden? Or, failing that, why not just buy bags of topsoil from the garden center?

If only it were that easy. To begin with, you have no way of knowing what's really in those bags of topsoil. Calling something topsoil doesn't make it good garden soil. All *topsoil* means is that it was the uppermost layer of dirt somewhere. Was that "somewhere" a former cotton field sold off for development? Perhaps that soil is full of herbicides and pesticides, or all worn out from too many years of poor farming practices. Maybe it was never very good soil in the first place.

Even if it turned out to be rich soil from a fertile garden, it still wouldn't be a good choice for my container garden. In a container, topsoil compacts and the spaces between soil particles disappear. Compacted soil cannot receive, contain, or allow for the movement of enough water and air. The same soil that could fully nurture plants in an earth garden cannot nurture them as well in a container garden. It's not that container edibles won't grow in topsoil; it's just that they won't grow nearly as well as they could, because they're not getting enough water and air.

Vermiculite. Made from a form of mica rock. The ore is heated to 2,000°F (1,093°C), causing it to expand and creating within it spaces for air and water. A cubic foot of vermiculite, which itself weighs about 8 pounds, can hold 32 pounds of water — about 8 gallons. In addition to its air- and water-holding ability, vermiculite provides some potassium, calcium, and magnesium. It has a neutral pH.

Perlite. Made from volcanic rock that is crushed, screened, and then heated to 1,800°F (982°C), causing the particles to expand. The result looks like zillions of tiny pieces of popcorn. Perlite holds water on its surface and keeps soil light and fluffy. It adds no nutrients to the mix and has a neutral pH.

Limestone (either dolomitic or calcitic). A source of calcium added to container mixes to counteract the acidity of peat moss. In addition to calcium, dolomitic limestone contains some magnesium.

If you're going to be gardening in self-watering containers, you'll want the main ingredient to be sphagnum peat, rather than sedge peat or coir. Sphagnum peat wicks water as well as sedge peat or coir, but doesn't hold as much water; it is therefore not as likely to become waterlogged. If, on the other hand, you're planning to grow vegetables in a traditional container, sedge peat or coir is a better choice because they can hold more water. You should also expect to see vermiculite or perlite (sometimes both) and some form of calcium — dolomitic or calcitic limestone or oyster shells — to counteract the acidity of the peat. At this stage of my search, that's all I want. No fertilizers, nothing to provide nutrition to my plants. All I'm interested in now is making sure they get enough, but not too much, water and air.

▲ *Which mix to pick?* *The low-quality potting mix on the left is full of twigs and wood chunks. The higher-quality mix on the right has noticeably more perlite and vermiculite, which makes the mix more evenly porous and allows for better movement of air and water.*

Don't Buy a Pig in a Poke

Before you make your purchase, try to find out what's inside the various bags of mix you've identified as potential keepers based on their ingredients. Not all kinds of peat are of the same quality. Some mixes keep the price down by scrimping on vermiculite and perlite, which cost more than peat. There's usually a reason why the less expensive mix is less expensive. Direct comparisons reveal the most. Look for even particle size in the peat, without a lot of twigs or chunks of wood. Cheaper mixes will also have more peat dust instead of full shreds of peat. A mix that has relatively more perlite (easy to spot) and/or vermiculite (not so easy — look for little golden flecks) is better than one with less.

WHAT YOU DON'T WANT IN A MIX

I always check the list of ingredients for any mix I plan to use for growing food because sometimes I find things that I don't want to end up in my soil. I'm gardening organically, so I don't want any synthetic fertilizers. Because most of my containers are self-watering, I also don't want any additives to increase water retention. These are called hydrogels, and they're meant to be used in traditional pots, which dry out quickly. When they're added to the potting mix in self-watering containers, the mix quickly becomes waterlogged. In short, I just want the basics — sphagnum peat, limestone, vermiculite, and/or perlite — and nothing else.

MY SECRET SOIL FORMULA

Container soils I've mixed myself and ready-made container soils that I've trialed successfully follow a simple recipe:

- One 20-quart bag of mature, high-quality compost
- One 20-quart bag of homemade or ready-made planting mixture (sphagnum peat, vermiculite or perlite, and limestone)

Depending on the quality of the compost, and perhaps on the appetite of the plants you're growing, you'll most likely need to supplement the mix with additional nutrients. In trials over the past three years, I have had success growing some kinds of vegetables for a whole season without additional fertilizer. But, to

▼ *Stirring soil. If you add a natural fertilizer to your potting soil, be sure to mix all ingredients thoroughly.*

err on the side of caution, you'll probably want to add the following organic fertilizer mix to your compost-based potting soil:

- ⅓ cup blood meal (for nitrogen)
- ⅓ cup colloidal phosphate (for phosphorus)
- ⅓ cup greensand (for potassium and trace elements)
- 1 tablespoon azomite

I empty all components (including the fertilizer mix) into a wheelbarrow and mix them together with a handheld cultivator. After the parts are combined, I moisten the soil with a steady stream from the garden hose as I continue to stir with the cultivator. The finished mix should be thoroughly moist but not sopping wet.

Bring on the Chow

Whether store-bought or homemade, any of the planting mixes we've talked about will ensure that our plants get the mix of air and water they need; we're starting with a sufficiently holey mix. But we're only halfway to a fruitful container medium. In addition to air and water, plants require certain kinds of food in certain amounts.

Plants need fairly large amounts of some nutrients, called *macronutrients.* Carbon, hydrogen, and oxygen come to a plant from air and water. The rest come from the soil. Nitrogen (the key element in chlorophyll, which enables the plant to do photosynthesis; nitrogen is also involved in protein synthesis), phosphorus (encourages root growth, increases disease resistance, and promotes development of flowers, fruits, and seeds), and potassium (involved in starch formation and increases resistance to stress and disease) are the most important of these. They are the nutrients referred to by the N-P-K percentages listed on bags of fertilizer. Other, secondary nutrients — calcium, magnesium, and sulfur — and *micronutrients* (needed just as much as macronutrients, but in much smaller amounts) boron, copper, iron, manganese, molybdenum, and zinc also perform vital functions in plant growth.

Much of modern agriculture, many earth gardeners, and many container gardeners meet their plants' needs very simply: by adding a balanced synthetic fertilizer. A balanced fertilizer contains equal amounts of the three nutrients — nitrogen (N), phosphorus (P), and potassium (K) — that plants require in the largest amounts. It's not a one-time proposition, however. Every week or so, more needs to be added. That's simple and easy, but it doesn't really work very well. Part of the problem is that synthetic fertilizers, while they do contain the macronutrients plants need, do not contain all of the secondary nutrients.

All of these nutrients, however, tend to be present in good garden soil in sufficient amounts. As it turns out, good soil has more to offer a plant than most gardeners realize. Good soil not only makes it possible for a plant to get enough water and air; it also contains the food a plant needs and provides the means by which it assimilates everything it needs for growth.

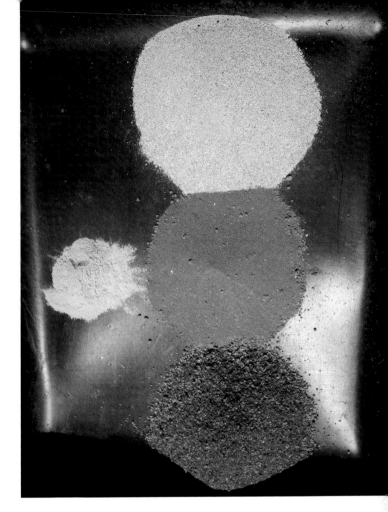

▲ *Pile it on!* Clockwise from left: *Azomite, colloidal phosphate, greensand, and blood meal make an excellent, slow-release fertilizer.*

The Importance of pH

Soil pH, indicated by a number between 1 and 14, is a measurement of acidity or alkalinity. Soil with a pH of 7.0 is neutral, neither acid nor alkaline; a pH below 7.0 is acid, above 7.0 is alkaline. Soil pH is important because some essential plant nutrients become unavailable if the soil is too acidic and other nutrients become unavailable if the soil is too alkaline. Most garden plants do best when the soil pH is between 6.0 and 7.0, although carrots, corn, eggplants, and potatoes can tolerate a pH of around 5.5; cabbage and cauliflower grow well at a pH of up to 7.5.

▲ *Good garbage*. *All kinds of green waste from your kitchen and garden can be added to a compost heap.*

Compost is Key

The key to creating a soil (for earth gardens or containers) that can accomplish all this is compost. Compost is the elixir that makes a living soil, a mixture of soil-dwelling creatures and the food upon which they depend. In other words, the decayed organic matter that we call compost is made up largely of soil microbes, bacteria, and fungi. Decomposing microbes eat organic matter and essentially make it part of themselves. What was a tomato leaf becomes bacteria; what was a particle of sawdust becomes fungi. The bacteria and fungi will, in turn, be eaten by predators, and their remains excreted. Adding compost to your container mix actually introduces a whole community of mutually dependent creatures that help to create the optimum conditions for plant growth.

Good compost has a number of other benefits:
- Compost greatly increases the water-absorbing and water-retaining capacity of soil, since it holds up to six times its weight in water.
- Compost increases the porosity of the soil, easing the movement of gases and dissolved minerals.

This means soil organisms can get the air they need and plant roots can get the nutrients they need.
- Compost provides many essential plant nutrients and the means to make those nutrients available in the right amounts and at the right time.
- Compost promotes plant growth by producing growth-stimulating hormones and chemicals.
- Compost moderates soil pH.
- Compost may help prevent some plant diseases.
- Compost is the primary and most important source of food for the living component of soil. Soil bacteria and fungi feed on compost, and protozoa, nematodes, earthworms, and many other creatures, large and small, feed on the bacteria and fungi.

Add to all of this the fact that making compost provides the ideal way to recycle organic material that otherwise would contribute to a massive rubbish disposal and pollution problem, and the word *miracle* really doesn't seem out of place. So, how do I make this miraculous stuff, this black gold?

Your Very Own Compost Heap

In a way, talking about "making compost" misses the point, because we gardeners can't *make* compost; all we can do is be helpful to the creatures that *do*. Those creatures are largely invisible to the naked eye; they are countless microbes, mostly bacteria and fungi. They're the ones that do the real work, consuming and digesting complex organic matter and reducing it to the simple nutrients that plants turn into complex organic matter. We are not compost makers; we are microbe farmers making sure that our invisible critters have a good place to live and the right sorts of food to eat.

Wanted — Warm, Moist, Airy House

Sooner or later, the creatures that make organic matter into compost will achieve their goal. We can help make it sooner rather than later if we provide an environment where many, many compost makers want to live and multiply. That's an environment that is moist — not sopping wet, but definitely moist. It's an environment that is warm; very few compost-making microbes are active below 50°F (10°C), and there isn't much going on until temperatures reach into the 70s. The real action starts to happen at around 100°F (38°C) and on up to 150°F (65°C) or so. Finally, there must be air. Compost-making organisms need to take in oxygen and they need to give off carbon dioxide.

The compost farm is a pile of organic material that is moist (but not wet) and warm, and has plenty of room for air to move in and out. As "compost farmers," we take organic matter that is thinly distributed over a wide area and may be too moist or not moist enough, and we concentrate it in one place. That is, we make a compost pile.

Will Work for Food

Rot happens. And it will happen faster if the ones doing the rotting work get a balanced diet — they'll eat more, multiply faster, and then eat even more. For a composting microbe, the "right foods" are mostly carbon and nitrogen, and the right amounts are roughly 30 servings of carbon to 1 of nitrogen. Compost farmers usually refer to carbon-rich materials as *browns* and nitrogen-rich materials as *greens*. The browns are not all brown, but many of them are: hay, dried pea and bean vines, straw, fallen leaves of autumn, sawdust. The greens are fresh plant matter, kitchen waste — parings, leftover salad greens, pea pods, the outer leaves of cabbages — and lawn clippings, weeds, thinnings from a row of carrots. Pond weeds and seaweed, which also contain trace minerals that plants may need, are also greens.

▶ *All worms welcome! Your compost bin will quickly become a haven for worms, which help turn green waste into finished compost.*

Pile It On

A compost pile is a warm, moist, airy microbe house made of food. Start with a three- or four-inch layer of coarse browns, like straw, that will allow air into the pile from the bottom. Then add some greens: use about an inch if the materials are compact, like kitchen scraps and lawn clippings, and three to six inches if the materials are loose, like pea vines and bean plants. Then layer more browns and greens and so on until you run out of material or room. Water the layers as you go: the browns are dry to begin with, so they'll need more water than the greens, which, although they may not be wet on the outside, contain mostly water on the inside.

▼ *Work it! Turn your compost pile frequently to increase air circulation and speed decomposition.*

If you get it right, the compost pile will shortly start to heat up. As this happens, a new batch of heat-loving microbes will start to take over the work. They work fast and they give off more heat, and then they multiply and work even faster. The result of all this heating and eating is a *hot pile*. If you can, make your compost in a hot pile; it's faster, and the high temperatures kill off any pathogenic organisms that might be in or on the composted materials. But if you don't have just the right amounts of greens and browns available at the right times, don't let that stop you. Compost still happens as long as the pile is neither too wet nor too dry and has enough air passing through it. Randomly arranged compost piles take longer to decompose, but the end result is just as good. (*Note:* If you want to compost the manures of any herbivores, like horses, cows, and chickens, a hot pile is recommended to kill any weed seeds the manure might contain.)

Containing the Pile

If you pile it, it will rot. In theory, that's all there is to it. In practice, you may need to put the pile *in* something. If you have plenty of room and can find a place where neither you nor anyone else finds an unruly compost pile objectionable, then just pile it up. To make a neater pile, contain it within a bin. You can make one from scrap wood or discarded pallets or you can buy ready-made wood, wire-mesh, or plastic containers. If you have close neighbors, or if there are wild or domestic animals that might want to feed on or otherwise mess with your pile, a plastic or metal bin may be best. Gardeners without much room at all can use a small plastic bin. A cover for the pile or the bin is a good idea, because it prevents both overwatering from rain and drying from evaporation.

This information should be enough to get you started on your compost adventure, but there's more to learn once you get hooked on having your own compost farm. The books listed in the appendix will give you further information.

How to Evaluate Store-Bought Compost

I make most of the compost I use in my earth garden, but even with access to a lot of organic materials to compost, I can't make nearly enough. If you can make any compost, do it; even if you don't make enough for your whole garden, any that you do make recycles that much organic matter and keeps it on the Great Wheel of Being rather than locked away in a landfill. That said, chances are that you'll have to buy at least some of the compost you need for your container garden; if you don't have a place to make even a little compost, you may have to buy *all* the compost you need.

When you make your own compost, you know what went into it, and you know how it was made. If you're buying compost, how do you know what it was made from? How do you know if it will be good for your container garden? As organic gardening has become more popular, many garden centers are selling compost or compost-based planting mixes. Usually the compost is in bags, but sometimes there's a big pile of it from which you can fill your own buckets, bags, or pickup truck. Many seed and garden-supply catalogs sell compost. Unfortunately, not all of the brown stuff labeled *compost* is of the same quality. There are presently no clear standards and no labeling laws to ensure that what's called compost really is compost, or that it is at least of a certain quality. Buyer beware. Or better perhaps to say, "Buyer be *aware*" — that is, be aware of what to look for in compost. Bagged or piled, by truck, by rail, or by mail, how do I know that I am getting good compost?

How Does It Look?

Good compost doesn't look like anything in particular. It doesn't, for instance, look like any of the various things it used to be before it became compost. You shouldn't be able to identify grass or leaves or plant parts. You shouldn't encounter large pieces of bark or twigs. The compost should be uniform in texture, moderately loose, and not lumpy. If there are a few lumps, they should crumble easily. Good compost is dark brown, sometimes almost black.

How Does It Smell?

Good compost should smell good: earthy and slightly pungent, like garden soil or the duff covering the forest floor. It should not stink. It shouldn't smell like manure or any sort of rotten stuff. It shouldn't be musty. Any pronounced unpleasant odor is a sign that something is not right.

CERTIFICATION

The labels on some of the compost you see for sale may indicate that the compost has been "certified" by some organization. What the certification means, what tests were done on the compost, and how the results were interpreted all vary depending on the certifying organization. If the label doesn't tell you what the certification means, contact the certifying organization; the easiest route is likely to be the Internet.

At this time, there is no single, nationally recognized certifying organization and there are no generally accepted guidelines for testing. The fact that a particular compost is not certified does not necessarily mean that it is not worthy of certification; it can mean that the maker has not applied for certification. At this stage of the compost market, a well-known brand name is a better guarantee of quality than an unknown certification.

GO LOCAL WITH COMPOST

Like your home compost heap, industrial compost makers include a variety of ingredients in their products. Much of the time, the wastes they include are those that are easiest (and least expensive) to come by. Compost operations based in suburban areas are likely to contain mostly yard waste — grass clippings, hedge trimmings, and leaves. In some municipal districts, large composting operations may even include dung from the zoo!

The contents of your store-bought compost will also vary by region. Gardeners in dairy country can usually find compost made from rotted cow manure (an excellent source of nitrogen). One company based in Maine collects and composts seaweed, spent blueberries, and waste from the shellfishing industry (ground-up crustacean shells have the unexpected benefit of helping the soil retain water). A charitable organization in Wisconsin uses a specific blend of waste matter from local industries, including duck litter, cranberries, rice hulls, wood shavings, pickles, and vanilla beans.

Is It Hot?

Compost that is warmer than the ambient temperature is not yet "finished." It may *become* good compost, but it's not there yet. Compost-making microbes give off heat as they digest organic matter, so the presence of heat is a sign that those microbes are still at work and need more time to finish the job of turning green waste into available nutrients. Until the heat subsides, the compost is not a good home for plants.

What Was It Made Of?

Good compost is diverse compost; it is made of many kinds of organic matter, the remains of many kinds of plants, the leaves of different trees, the manures of various barnyard critters, seaweeds, fish, alfalfa, wheat straw, poultry feathers — the more, the merrier. The more different things that go into a compost mix, the more varied the microbial population that feeds on it. And the more varied the microbial population, the greater the chance that it will contain the particular communities of microbes that best suit the plants you want to grow.

What went into the heap at the beginning of the process will also affect the nutrient level of the finished compost. A pile of rotting manure and chopped straw, for instance, will result in compost with much more nitrogen than a pile of leaf mold. Compost that has rotting manure as its base will therefore be better able to give container plants what they need to grow and thrive.

Sometimes the ingredients of compost will be listed on the bag or in the catalog description. Sometimes the people selling the compost will know what went into it. If you know or can find out who made the compost, you can ask what went into it. Unless there is no other option, I don't like to buy compost whose lineage is a mystery. Whatever is in there will eventually end up as part of my food.

What Was It *Not* Made Of?

There are definitely a few things that should not be in compost. Heavy metals and chemicals toxic to either plants or people don't belong in compost. Composted sewage sludge sometimes contains these toxins and therefore is not recommended by most organic organizations. Herbicides and pesticides are also potential dangers. Some of them break down during the composting process and lose their effectiveness, but some don't. In a study done by Pennsylvania State University, at least one of the major herbicides commonly used on suburban lawns — clopyralid — retained its effectiveness, even after being composted. If a compost includes lawn clippings, make sure that it has been tested and is guaranteed not to contain herbicides.

Ask Around

Are there any organic gardeners or farmers in your neighborhood? What compost do they use? Where do they get it? Why does the garden center sell one compost and not another? Do any local nurseries use compost or a compost-based planting mix? Where do they get it? Is there any compost sold by your favorite seed company? Its reputation depends on what it sells; it can't afford to have poor quality in either seeds or compost. When all else fails, check the Internet.

I'm lucky — there's a commercial compost maker less than half an hour away from where I live. I've been to visit, and have met the maker and seen how the compost is made and what goes into it. I've asked for references and talked to farmers and gardeners who use that compost. I have a pretty good idea of what sort of compost I'm buying.

▲ *Gardener's gold. Good compost is dark and friable.*

CHAPTER FOUR

TOOLS AND ACCESSORIES

Container gardeners don't have any use for most of the tools in the earth gardener's shed, though the shed itself might come in handy for storing containers and potting mix over the winter. Most of what a container gardener needs by way of tools can fit in an apron or a small basket or tote.

Gloves

Although I garden mostly bare-handed, I sometimes use gloves for mixing and moistening container soil. Otherwise, those jobs can leave me with chapped and abraded hands.

There are generally three options in the world of gloves — waterproof, semi-waterproof, and not-at-all waterproof. The thoroughly waterproof gloves are made of fabric dipped in something like rubber. I use these gloves for mixing and moistening container-soil ingredients. The semi-waterproof gloves are of fabric but have been coated on the palm half with rubber or some rubberlike substance. If you're up to your wrists in water, these won't keep your hands dry, but you can muck about in damp soil — transplanting, for instance — without getting wet or cold fingers. Just plain fabric gloves dampen quickly in moist soil; they're really just for keeping your hands clean while you're tending, pruning, and harvesting.

▲ *Handy tools. Many of these tools are not strictly necessary for container gardeners, but I think they come in handy for certain tasks. Left to right: Pruning shears, trowels, a soil scoop, floral scissors, and a cultivator (for mixing soil).*

Trowels

Most garden trowels are too big for container gardening. Container soil is loose and friable and designed to stay that way; it is, therefore, easier to dig a hole in container soil than in most garden soils, and I don't need the extra leverage provided by a big tool. Often the only digging tool I use is the "trowel" at the end of my wrist, perhaps protected by a glove. Using a proper trowel sometimes just slows me down. When I do use a trowel, I prefer a smaller one than I'd typically use in my earth garden.

Pruning, Thinning, and Harvesting

I do most of my pruning and a lot of the leaf harvesting for salad with that same multipurpose tool I use in place of a trowel: my hand. The "hand tool" in this case is my thumbnail pressed against my index finger. This works just fine (if I haven't trimmed my thumbnail too short), but I do end up with a "green thumb."

Floral Scissors

If I don't want to have a literally green thumb, and when I've remembered to bring them with me to the container garden, I prune, harvest, and thin with floral scissors. The sharp points of the scissors let me get into tight spaces without damaging adjacent plants or foliage. I use the same scissors for pruning suckers from tomato plants, removing damaged leaves or broken stems, thinning carrots or beets, and harvesting greens.

Serrated Knife

For harvesting mature lettuce or pak choi, a serrated knife works well. Stick with a cheap hardware-store version, though, not one of your good kitchen knives. Contact with soil will dull any knife fairly quickly.

Pruning Shears

These tend to be too cumbersome for delicate work like pruning or thinning; they can crush rather than cut tender stems. But they're very effective for harvesting squashes and pumpkins and for lopping off mature plants at the end of the season and cutting them into pieces for the compost bin or pile.

Harvest Basket

A sturdy basket can hold the tools, seed packets, garden books, and whatever else I'll need for a pleasant morning working with my plants. And when it's time for lunch, there's room for squash, cucumbers, some greens for salad, and a handful of beans.

▲ *Harvest help.* Top to bottom: *Floral scissors work well for snipping herbs and edible flowers. A serrated knife is the perfect tool for harvesting heads of cabbage. This harvest basket (made by my son, Nathan) is just the right size for picking vegetables for dinner.*

Watering

Vegetable plants growing in any sort of container need a lot of water; natural rainfall will not provide anywhere near enough. The fruitfulness and beauty of your container garden will depend on your supplying it with the considerable amount of water that nature can't deliver. The pleasure you have in your garden will depend on how easy it is for you to supply that water.

Hoses

Carrying water in a watering can for a large container garden will become wearying in a big hurry. Watering with a hose saves time and effort. Just as I can reach every bed in my earth garden with a hose, I can water every container in my container garden with a hose. I wouldn't have it any other way.

All other things — like sun exposure and aesthetic niceties — being equal, I put my container garden (or container gardens) as close as I can to the water faucet. Then I run a hose or hoses (I have three large container gardens some distance apart) all the way to the farthest containers. I hide the hose as well as I can so it doesn't call attention to itself, but it is there all the time, and is essential to my contentment in the garden.

If you don't have an outdoor faucet to hook up a garden hose, you can buy a specially designed coiled hose that attaches to an indoor faucet and run it outside through an open window or door. These generally have a switch at the handle end to turn the water on and off, which makes watering *only* the container — and not the rest of the patio — that much easier.

Coiled Hose Extension

I am amazed, sometimes, at the amount of destruction I can leave in my wake if I become inattentive for a few minutes as I drag a heavy hose from container to container. A coiled hose is neither very heavy nor very cumbersome and makes the job of watering as near to pleasant as it can be. Stretched out, it reaches all my containers; coiled, it occupies only a small space.

Watering Cans

A good watering can for self-watering containers should have a spout small enough to fit in various fill holes and fill tubes. If the soil in a self-watering container ever dries on the surface, you'll need to water the soil surface from above before adding water to the reservoir. To do that, your watering can should have an accessory rose.

As a rule, I favor old-time tools made of old-time materials, but my favorite container watering can, though of a classic Hawes design, is made of plastic. It weighs less than a metal can, it won't rust, and it can suffer considerable abuse without developing a leak. The Hawes design makes for a well-balanced tool with a comfortable handle; the long spout means I can water many of my containers standing up.

The spout is small enough to fit where it needs to fit. An accessory spout directs the water at right angles. This is handy for getting water into container fill tubes. The accessory rose has many small holes and can be used with the holes upward, resulting in a fine, rainlike spray that moistens container soil very effectively.

◀ *Homemade and handy. I created this handy hose attachment by simply cutting a washing-machine hose in two and attaching one end to a pistol-grip sprayer. The hose end is flexible and fits nicely into the fill hole.*

The business end of the hose is too big to fit inside the fill holes or fill tubes of many self-watering containers. To solve that problem, we have tried a number of ways to make watering easier.

▲ *Easy watering. We bought this funnel from a gas station and attached it to the container with plastic ties.*

Some watering cans are narrow enough to fit inside the fill hole. At least one gardener we know has used a funnel to direct water into the container (as pictured above). Our own solution is to use a hose with a pistol-grip attachment that has been connected to half of a washing-machine hose (shown at left).

Monitoring and Measuring

I like to know as much as I can about what's going on in the air and the soil of the garden. The more I know, the better chance I have of understanding the outcomes, good and not so good. But it's not just that my outcomes may be better as a result. Part of the fun of gardening is just in getting to know my garden.

Min-Max Thermometer

A regular thermometer can tell me how warm or cold it is right now. And right now, as I write, the regular thermometer says it's 65°F (18°C) outside. That's fine and dandy as far as basil is concerned, so it may be time to transplant the basil from the warm confines of my porch to the "real world" of an outdoor container. But I also know that basil can be set back in its growth if the night temperatures go below 40°F (4°C). My regular thermometer would have told me if temperatures were that low last night — but I wasn't awake to be told! That's why I have a min-max thermometer. Last night it recorded that the temperature dropped to 37°F (3°C) — cold enough that I'd better wait to transplant that basil.

Soil Thermometer

When I read in part three that lettuce seeds germinate best below 60°F (15°C), that's not the *air* temperature we're talking about; it's the *soil* temperature. My regular thermometer tells me the air temperature. If I want to measure soil temperature, I need a soil thermometer.

A regular thermometer in the shade will read differently from one in full sun. Similarly, a soil thermometer pushed an inch into the soil may differ significantly from one placed three inches deeper. I get meaningful readings on a soil thermometer only when I'm comparing readings from the same soil depth.

◄ *Degrees of difference. A soil thermometer can help you plant picky vegetables when the soil reaches their desired temperature.*

Seed Catalogs: A Favorite Garden Tool

Oh? A seed catalog is a tool? Yep. It's the tool I use to pick out what I'll grow in my container garden. Like any tool, there are good ones and ones that are pretty much worthless. I like seed catalogs that help me make good choices for container growing, since a plant variety that's perfect for an earth garden may be a poor choice for a container. I can't assume that my list of Golden Oldies will play as sweetly in a new dance hall. So what am I looking for in a catalog that will help me find what I want in a container vegetable?

At the top of my list is a good, complete description. How tall is the plant, how wide does it spread? How long does it take to mature? Is it susceptible to any diseases or bothered by any pests? How does it taste? Is this plant in any way strikingly attractive? Color? Texture of the leaves? Does it have pretty flowers? Is it easy to grow or a bit fussy?

Some catalogs will tell me all of that and more. Others tell me almost nothing.

A picture is worth a thousand words, it's said. And in this case, at least, it's true: it's much easier to imagine a lettuce garden if I have pictures before my eyes. Don't *tell me* about red, let me *see* red. What do you mean, for instance, by "burgundy"? If I have a picture, I don't have to wonder if the catalog writer has the same burgundy in mind that I do.

Some catalogs — more and more each year — will identify, with words or icons, which plants should do well in containers. But you can also spot good container candidates on your own by watching for some key words in the plant description: "compact" plants will take up less container room than normal plants of that same variety, as will ones with an "upright growth habit"; "bush" or "semi-bush" varieties will take less space and wander around the neighborhood less wantonly (though you should keep in mind that even bush varieties may meander some, so you can't assume that the plant will be entirely docile).

▲ *Grow up!* The entrance to our container garden (above) is marked by self-watering planters connected by an arbor of scarlet runner beans (top left). In another planter, cucumbers grow up a trellis (middle left). Sometimes, a cage is needed to keep tomatoes in bounds (bottom left).

Training and Support

Some edible plants need to climb: peas and pole beans, for instance, are not content to crawl along the ground. Tomatoes and cucumbers can either climb or crawl, but they take up less space and generally grow better if they have some sort of support to grow on. Anything from a single stake to an elaborate arch can provide that support and may, along the way, add some beauty to the garden.

Trellises and Stakes

In an earth garden, trellises can be pretty simple; just a wooden stake driven into the ground will suffice for tomatoes. Three long poles anchored in the ground make a tepee for beans. Two poles in the ground connected by netting or chicken wire support peas or beans. But in a container garden, things are not so easy. Container soil is much looser and lighter than garden soil, and it isn't as deep. Often, wooden stakes in container soil can barely support *themselves,* let alone a heavy tomato plant.

In a container, plant supports usually need to be attached to the container itself or to something sturdy nearby, or they must be driven deep into the soil outside the container (provided your container is resting directly on the ground and not on a deck or patio). Some kinds of containers are sold with accessory trellises that attach through holes in the container. Tomato cages, because they are largely supported by their bottom crossbars resting on the soil surface, work as well in containers as they to do in the garden.

▲ *Keep movin'.* A wheeled dolly will make even a very heavy container portable. We use ours to move pots inside when a frost threatens.

Transportation

When empty, all but the largest containers are light enough to carry around. But filled with moist soil, water, and plants, all but the smallest are too heavy for most of us to move alone. If you can, place containers where they'll be for the whole growing season. If you need to move them later to get better exposure to sunlight or protection from frost, for instance, plan on having helpers with strong backs. Or if your containers will be on a fairly smooth surface like a deck or patio, equip them with wheels.

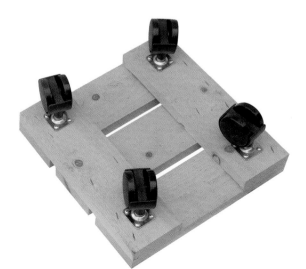

PART TWO

Putting It All Together

CHAPTER FIVE

GETTING STARTED

There you sit on a sunny spring day, dreams of sugarplums dancing in your head. Well, maybe not sugarplums — more like salads and salsa, peppers and onions, radishes and peas. How do you get from culinary fantasies to container-garden realities? How do you turn the promise of spring into the harvest of summer?

Start Small

I often give myself very good advice and very seldom take it. My often given and seldom taken garden advice is to start small and doable instead of big and impossible. In the hopes that you are wiser than I, let me suggest that your first container garden be small. Start with just a few containers growing plants you're pretty sure will do well and not require much fussing.

Most of the time, container gardening is less work than earth gardening. Containers need little weeding and no cultivating. Container plants are also less likely than earth garden plants to be bothered by pests or diseases. But container gardens need to be watered more often than earth gardens — a lot more often. That watering takes time, and it needs to be done regularly and without fail. Self-watering containers usually allow more time between waterings than traditional containers, but they still need regular attention. Every container you add to your garden increases the amount of time you'll need to spend watering.

In the earth garden, there is some margin for error. You can sometimes get away with not watering at the moment you ought to. Not so in the container garden — when container plants don't have enough water, the whole show comes to a screeching halt. That tomato plant covered in bright red tomatoes and dancing in your dreams needs about a gallon of water every single day. Five tomato plants will need about five gallons. A gallon of water weighs eight pounds, more or less. You want your garden to be productive, but you also want it to be fun and to allow room in your life for other things in the time you have away from work. Start small. Let the garden gradually expand to fill the time you really have to spend gardening, the time you really want to spend gardening. This is, after all, supposed to be enjoyable.

What Does Your Garden Grow?

Fine. You've promised that you won't try to grow everything in the seed catalog. (Not *this* year, anyway.) So you have to make some choices. From the hundreds of vegetables available at the local nursery or from seed catalogs, how do you choose?

Edibles That Taste Best When Just Picked

Cucumbers, peppers, and onions bought at a farmer's market or even at the grocery store may be a bit less tasty than what I could pick from my own garden, but just a bit less, provided, of course, that the purchased food was grown well in the first place. Some edibles taste "fresh picked" for a while after harvest and don't really need to be absolutely fresh to be tasty. But peas, beans, small and tender-skinned summer squash, vine-ripened tomatoes — all picked moments before eating — are in another league entirely from the "garden fresh" produce in a market. The same goes for lettuces, spinach, and salad greens of any kind. For some edibles, there is no substitute for fresh picked. I'll therefore grow peas before I'll grow onions, summer squash rather than winter squash, and filet beans or eggplant sooner than cabbage.

When planning your container garden, think about what you're going to get in return for your investment. In the same space, for about the same amount of work, you can grow one tomato plant from which you can expect to harvest 20 or 30 pounds of tomatoes (maybe more). Or one artichoke plant from which you may harvest half a dozen artichokes (probably less). Or you can fill a container with mixed greens from which you'll harvest almost daily all the salad greens you can eat. Or you can grow a summer squash plant from which you can have a steady supply of fresh squash. Or you can grow 18 onions.

▲ *Fresh from the garden. There's nothing fresher than a salad harvested just minutes before lunch from a container on the front porch.*

If you have enough containers and enough time, you may choose to grow an artichoke plant. Personally, I wouldn't grow an artichoke plant instead of a tomato or a pattypan squash plant. And I'd rather have a mess of salad greens than I would a few onions.

All life depends on solar energy. For most living things, that is a dilemma, because most living things cannot utilize solar energy directly. We depend on solar energy, but we do not have the means to capture and use it. But green plants do.

Green plants, like the ones we'll be growing in our gardens, can do what no other living things can: capture solar energy and convert it into forms they can use. This captured solar energy can then be consumed by plant-eating creatures and, in turn, by the creatures that consume them. The process by which plants capture solar energy is called *photosynthesis* — literally, "putting together with light."

Green plants use photons of solar energy to break apart molecules of water and molecules of carbon dioxide and combine the liberated hydrogen and carbon into carbohydrates, the basic building blocks of life. Our first task, then, as gardeners, is to make sure that our plants have the best possible chance to capture solar energy and work their photosynthetic miracle. You can't have photosynthesis without the photo part.

Varieties the Grocery Store Doesn't Sell

My first priority is to grow the food I can't have unless I grow it myself. That means growing edibles that taste best when fresh picked, but it also means looking for varieties that can't be found at the grocery store. Most often, the commercially raised vegetables are chosen for reasons other than taste — because they ship well without bruising or because they can store for long periods without going bad. But the best-tasting tomato is often not the one that can stand a cross-country trip. As container gardeners, we have the opportunity to explore new and delicious foods by growing them ourselves. A whole new avenue for appetite can be opened! I've tried growing many of the edibles you see in seed catalogs, and make recommendations for particular varieties in part three of this book.

Playing the Hand You're Dealt

When choosing your edibles, you will also need to consider how much sun your potential garden spot receives. If the sun shines brightly most of the day over most of your yard or deck or patio, you can grow pretty much whatever you choose. But if the sunniest spot you have is sunny for only a few hours each day, you're asking for heartbreak if you try to grow tomatoes there, or eggplants, or any other plant that needs lots and lots of sun.

If your container-garden site gets very warm and does so fairly early in the year, lettuce and spinach are not going to like that. You'll be better off planning summer salads of tetragonia or some other heat-tolerant greens.

Location Matters

Where does my (container) garden go? Or, perhaps more to the point, where do my garden*s* go? A container garden has the advantage over an earth garden because it is made up of many small and movable pieces, each a sort of garden in itself. Those pieces can be here, there, and almost anywhere. Container gardeners have a lot more flexibility about garden location than do earth gardeners.

Consider the Sun

My first garden, planted more years ago than I choose to count, was largely a disaster. I harvested two radishes and three carrots. The largest carrot was four inches long; the other two were two inches long. I had planted my garden in the shade of a cedar grove. I didn't entirely understand what had happened, but I

▲ *A place in the sun. Squash and celery need full sun to grow to their full potential.*

did manage to make the connection between my sparse harvest and the absence of sun in my garden. I've made many mistakes in gardening since, but I haven't made that one again. The three most important things to consider when I'm deciding what containers go where in my container garden? Sun, sun, and sun.

Some plants — hostas, for instance — need very little sun; they're considered shade lovers. But there are no shade lovers among the plants we grow as edibles. There are some, called shade tolerant, that need less sun than others, but all the plants we'll grow in our container gardens need some sun, and most need at least six hours of unobstructed sunlight every day. Even plants that will tolerate some shade grow faster and produce better if they get more sunlight. Plants with a more tropical heritage, like tomatoes, need at least eight hours of sunlight. If you have more containers than you have sunny places, be sure to dole out the sunniest spots to the plants that need them most.

Tomatoes, peppers, eggplants, and other plants that come from warm, sunny climates, as well as big plants like corn and squash, all need lots of sun. But some littler folks need a place in the sun too. Onions, garlic, and carrots have very little surface area to their foliage. Photosynthesis happens only where the sun meets the green; if there's not much green surface area, there's not much photosynthesis. Because of that, onions, garlic, and carrots, although they'll survive okay in partial sun, will grow bigger if they grow in full sunlight. They're not alone. Most vegetable plants do better with more sun — a minimum of six hours a day.

Is There a Shade Lover in the House?

Nonetheless, there are some vegetables that will suffer less than others if they don't get access to full sun. If you have to choose, these shade-tolerant plants can be handed the short end of the sun ration. Lettuces are shade tolerant, as is spinach. These plants and others listed in the box at left consist mostly of leaves. They have relatively large expanses of leaf surface for photosynthesis and relatively small plants to grow with the products of that photosynthesis. Even shade-tolerant edibles, however, grow faster and yield a bigger crop with more sun, provided the extra sunlight does not increase soil temperature too much.

Shorten the Water Haul

If you have enough sunny places for the plants you want to grow, the only roadblock on your way to a successful container garden is water. Without access to all the water they need, container plants won't grow well. Without easy access to that water, the container gardener won't have much fun.

One end of hose is a lot easier to move from container to container than a watering can that weighs upward of 15 pounds when full. Your garden chores will be easier and a lot more fun if most or all of your garden is within easy reach of a faucet that you can attach a hose to. If only part of your garden can be near water, put the plants that need the most water closest to the water source.

HOW MUCH SUN?

Not every vegetable needs the same amount of time in the sun. Many need full sun (at least six hours a day) to grow well, though some will tolerate less (four to six hours a day).

Plants that need full sun:

- artichokes
- basil
- bush beans
- celery
- cilantro (if grown for seed)
- corn
- cucumbers
- dill
- eggplant
- fennel
- marjoram
- melons
- okra
- peppers
- sweet potatoes
- squash
- tarragon
- tomatoes

Shade-tolerant plants:

- arugula
- cilantro (if grown for foliage)
- claytonia
- cress
- endive/escarole
- kale
- lettuces
- mustard
- radicchio
- orach
- oregano
- parsley
- sage
- spinach
- Swiss chard

One Size Doesn't Fit All

It depends on what I'm trying to grow, but as a general rule, I favor large containers. A relatively small herb plant, like basil, can grow alone in a fairly small container, but most of the plants I want to grow in my container garden are not small — or if they are, I usually want to grow many of them.

If I'm growing an indeterminate, full-size tomato, for instance, I want at least 20 quarts of soil, and a gallon of water storage will get that plant through only a day at the peak of its growth cycle. So a 30-quart container, with at least a third of that space for a reservoir, is the least I'll need. If I plan to be away for a weekend in August, two or more gallons of reserve in the reservoir is a good idea. Even a window-box lettuce garden will need a quart of water or more a day; a self-watering

▲ *Ciao, bambino! Eggplants usually need to be grown solo in large containers, but this cultivar, 'Bambino', does just fine in a medium-size pot with lettuce or small basil plants.*

container that can't provide that isn't really much of an improvement over a traditional container.

For serious food production, I prefer containers that hold about 40 quarts of soil and provide at least a couple of gallons of reservoir capacity. We do grow salad greens in smaller containers, but most of our pots are on the large side. When we do use window boxes or other smaller containers, we choose the ones with the largest reservoirs and the best water-to-soil ratios.

Large containers can support most full-size plants. Medium and small containers are better suited to compact plants. Except for plants with a long taproot, containers with eight inches of soil work well. Most kinds of carrots and beets need 10 to 12 inches of soil.

CHAPTER SIX

OF SEEDS AND SIX-PACKS

So, you have finally decided which edibles to grow. Some of your choices can go directly into the soil as seeds. Some need to start their container life as transplants. Starting your own plants allows you to grow uncommon varieties, but maybe you'd rather keep it simple and just buy plants. Here are a few tips to help you decide what to do and how to do it.

Buying Plants

Although Sylvia and I start seeds for most of the plants in our earth garden, we buy most of our container garden plants from local greenhouses. In our earth garden, most of the tomatoes we grow are destined for tomato juice and sauce; in the containers, all the tomatoes will be for fresh eating in salads and sandwiches or garden-fresh spaghetti sauce. The best varieties for canning and freezing are not usually the best for fresh eating. We may grow a dozen or even two dozen plants of one variety in the earth garden — this is all or most of the seeds in a packet. But in the containers, one each of two, three, or four varieties is what we're after — just one or two seeds from each packet. It's cheaper to buy one plant from a greenhouse than it is to buy a packet of seeds from which we use only a few. I've noticed that more and more seed catalogs are also selling "started plants" of tomatoes, peppers, and eggplants, including heirloom varieties.

▼ *Shop well. When choosing plants from a nursery or green- house, be sure to pick ones that are stocky, firm, and green. A bad start in life can lead to unhealthy plants later on.*

Garden Center Checklist

It is possible to buy healthy, well-started plants at a greenhouse or garden center; it is also possible to buy weak, sickly, and severely stressed plants that never amount to much and give very little return even after a summer of careful tending. Here's what to look for and what to avoid.

If you have the room to keep plants indoors and the time to tend them, do your shopping early in the season, at least two or three weeks before it is time to transplant outdoors. If the plants need to be repotted before they are ready to go into containers, you can do that yourself; the nurseries rarely have the time for this, so many of the plants sold near transplanting time are pot-bound. That is, their roots don't have enough room to grow and have turned inward instead of continuing to extend outward; pot-bound plants are stressed and will have difficulty establishing good root systems after they are transplanted. You can tell a plant is pot-bound when you see a mass of white roots matted together when you remove the plant from its container.

If you have the plants at home with you for most of their early life, you can be sure they will get the care they need when they need it. (If you can't buy your

plants as early as I suggest, do at least plan to get them home a week before you expect to plant so you can "harden them off" — that is, accustom them gradually to life outdoors. (See "Toughen Up," this page, for more about hardening off.)

Tip #1 Try to find plants in four-inch pots rather than in small pots or six-packs. The larger pot ensures that the seedling has enough soil to maintain a steady supply of moisture and nutrients while it's growing.

Tip #2 Choose short, bushy plants over tall, willowy ones. The tall ones have been starved for light; that's what they're stretching toward.

Tip #3 Avoid plants that have blossoms. In a young tomato, pepper, or eggplant, for example, blossoms are a sign not of health and vigor but of stress. It is way too early for a little plant with a tiny root system to be getting on with the job of setting and maturing fruit. Without the roots to supply water and food, the poor plant will produce few fruits, and only small ones. (If, by the time they are ready for transplanting to containers, any of your plants have blossoms, pluck them off. Give the plants time to grow roots.)

Tip #4 Look for stems and leaves that are deep green. Pale green or yellow leaves often indicate a nitrogen deficiency. A purple cast to older leaves points to a phosphorus deficiency.

Tip #5 Check the stems and the undersides of the leaves for aphids and other insects. Discolored, misshapen, or partially eaten leaves are an indication that all is not right with a plant. We gardeners usually have all the problems we need without importing more!

▲ *Bigger is better. Although most plants are sold in six-packs, you're better off buying plants in four-inch pots. A bigger pot holds more soil, which means that your plant is less likely to have suffered from drought stress.*

TOUGHEN UP!

Once you have your plants at home, begin the process of weaning them from the warm, cozy, and safe environment of the greenhouse. Life is going to get a bit iffy for the little plants, and they need to be prepared for some harsh realities.

Start by putting your charges outdoors in a shady spot away from the wind for an hour or so, then bring them back inside. On the second day, try two hours, then three on the third. As the plants get used to outdoor life, you can put them in the sun for a while, then back in the shade. Time the outings so the plants are ready for a full day outdoors in the sun by the time you want to transplant them to containers.

Try to transplant on a cloudy day, in the late afternoon or evening, so the tender plants won't have to cope right away with the heat of the day. If you must plant when it's sunny and/or windy, cover the transplants with a plastic pot for a day, or until conditions change. Water all seedlings thoroughly before and after planting.

1 With your fingers or a trowel, dig a hole a bit larger than the transplant's root-ball.

2 If the plant is in a cell, pop it out by pushing from below or by using a fork to lift the plant.

3 Place the root-ball in the hole and fill the remaining space with soil.

4 Pat the soil gently to eliminate any large gaps, but don't pack it down hard. Water well. One month later (pictured at left), the 'Eight-Ball' zucchini and 'Red Sails' lettuce are coming along nicely.

Starting from Seed

There are many reasons to grow your own plants from seed. If you start your own plants, you know exactly how they have been cared for. You know what sort of soil they've grown in, what they've had for food, whether they've been bothered by pests. You can move them to larger pots whenever they need more room.

Every plant in every garden starts from a seed, but the seed may start in the garden or indoors. Seeds that go right in the garden are mostly for plants that are difficult or even impossible to transplant. Or some just gain no particular advantage from starting earlier or in a protected environment. Seeds that start indoors are usually for plants that need a head start in order to produce a crop during a too-short outdoor growing season. Most of the rest get a better start indoors, where they are safe from pests and temperature fluctuations. And there are some — salad greens, for instance — that can start *either* in the garden or indoors. When a plant falls in that category, I start it indoors if I have the room and the time.

Bottom Heat

Some plants — melons, eggplants, and peppers, for instance — germinate more quickly and at a better rate at a fairly high soil temperature, as high as 80–90°F (26–32°C). I don't keep the house that warm, so I start seeds for heat-loving plants on a heating mat. (This is a plastic or rubber mat with a heating coil running through it.) When you plug it in and place your filled containers on top of it, the gentle heat from the mat warms the soil of the containers. Be careful to roll and unroll heating mats only when they are warm, to avoid cracking the plastic covering; a cracked mat quickly becomes an electrical hazard.

▲ *On their own. These lettuce seedlings have been recently transplanted into their own containers, to give them more room to grow.*

A SELF-WATERING SOLUTION

For most of the plants I start indoors, my favorite seed-starting containers are, like my favorite garden containers, self-watering (see page 64). The self-watering planter has a reservoir, capillary matting to serve as a wick, holes in the cell bottoms so the soil can be in contact with the wick, and a place for soil and plants. This starting system has the advantage of giving seedlings a consistent level of moisture; drought-stressed plants can be stunted and sickly. Most plants don't ever fully recover from abuse they suffer as seedlings.

Planting instructions on seed packets and seed catalogs often determine planting dates by reference to the "last frost date." That's the date when the last spring frost is likely to occur in the area where you live and garden. It's a guess based on when the last frost has occurred in years past.

But it doesn't take into account the microclimates in your state, in your town, or even in your neighborhood. I've even had frosts that affected one part of my garden while having no effect on the rest. So, what do you do?

▲ *Sweet greens. Kale is one of the few plants that actually taste better after a frost.*

First, check the "last frost date" map at the end of this book. Talk to your neighbors, especially your gardener neighbors. Check the long-range weather forecasts. Cast your lot. (And be prepared to cover or move containers with frost-sensitive plants if you've guessed wrong.)

TLC for Tiny Plants

Taking care of little seedlings isn't difficult, but it does require some planning and a lot of attention. Here are some suggestions for how to give your plantlets the best of everything:

LIGHT

Seedlings need light, and lots of it. Move them around if necessary from sunny spot to sunny spot so they get as much light as possible. Fluorescent lights will do the job better and go right on supplying light even on cloudy days. But they cost extra money, take up space, and use electricity. I make do with the sun and expect the growth process to take a little longer than it would under fluorescent lights. If you do use lights, keep them about three inches above the plants.

WATER

Seedlings are more sensitive than larger plants to fluctuations in their water supply. If you're using self-watering planters, check the reservoirs regularly. If you're using traditional planters, never let the soil dry out, even if you have to water more than once a day. Peat pots and soil blocks will dry out sooner than plastic pots and cells.

FOOD

Seedlings will need more or less fertilizer more or less frequently depending on the potting soil they live in. I have found that plants growing in a compost-based mix like the ones I use in garden containers do not need supplemental fertilizer. Plants growing in other mixes may need fertilizer once a week. Liquid fertilizers are the easiest to use; just water with a fertilizer mix instead of water when it's time to fertilize.

WARMTH

Most seedlings do well most of the time in warm, but not hot, temperatures. Some like a period of cooler temperatures. Some are stressed by cool temperatures. Check the preferred temperatures for growth of each edible in part three.

Getting a Head Start

Starting your own plants indoors isn't rocket science, and it needn't involve a lot of expensive equipment. You'll just need seeds, some starting mix, and something to put the seeds and soil into — a small container of some sort. Start small and simple and add to your seed-starting supplies as experience teaches you what you need.

Something to Sink Your Roots Into

You can see from any visit to any garden center that there are a number of ready-made mixes for starting seeds; they'll be labeled *germinating mix*, *transplanting mix*, or *seed-starting mix*. You probably can't go far wrong with any of them. I use the same mix in my starting containers that I use in garden containers. The plants start life in the very same soil they'll live in for the rest of their lives.

▲ *Get growing! Starting plants indoors can be a fun way to get a jump on the growing season. To make sure your seedlings get enough light, set them in front of a sunny, south-facing window.*

GERMINATION RATE The number of seeds that actually become plants out of the number of seeds you sow. For instance, if you plant 10 seeds but only 4 sprout, you have a 40 percent germination rate. Most seed packets indicate typical rates for each kind of plant. If the seeds you're using have a low germination rate, or if you're using old seeds, plant a few extras.

▲ *Hello, little sprout.* Beets should always be grown from seed, sown directly into the self-watering container.

Some planting mixes contain fertilizer and some don't. Those that do often contain very little, and thus will feed seedlings for only a short time. Read the labels so you'll know when and how to fertilize. (The mix I use contains fertilizer; but if you need to apply your own, I recommend using a liquid seaweed fertilizer.)

Something to Sink Your Soil Into

Starting plants indoors is a form of container gardening. And, just as I could use almost anything large that will hold soil as a large container, I could use just about anything small that will contain soil as a seed-starting container. Recycled Styrofoam coffee cups, tin cans, milk cartons cut in half, and yogurt containers — I've used them all, and they all work fine, more or less. You can also buy store-bought pots made of plastic or peat, or flats made of plastic or wood, sometimes divided into cells. I've tried many; they all work. Some seem to work better than others — less work, less mess, faster germination, stronger plants, or some combination of the above.

I usually fill my containers with transplants, but sometimes I have to start from seeds. The plants involved may be difficult or impossible to transplant, like carrots and beets, or they may be best grown in a dense planting like mesclun or a cut-and-come-again lettuce bed.

1 Make a furrow of about the right depth for the seeds you're planting, using a short length of wood. (Check part three for planting depths.)

2 Sow the seeds, spacing them according to the information in part three. In general, the bigger the seed, the deeper it goes.

3 Cover the seeds with moist soil. Crumble the soil as you go, ensuring that the soil particles are small and make good contact with the seeds. Gently tamp down the soil.

4 Water the seeds with a gentle shower from a watering can with a fine rose.

5 Label the row. (That's the part I always forget.)

In just a few weeks, the greens we planted will be a harvestable size.

CHAPTER SEVEN

DESIGNING FOR CONTAINERS

Planning a container vegetable garden can be a tricky business. Although you'll want it to look good, its main purpose is to produce food that tastes great — and those two goals do not always coincide. Some vegetables might look good together but not grow well together. With some planning, though, a container can be both beautiful and productive.

A Tasteful Aesthetic

A summer squash flower is, as a flower, gorgeous, a morning glory — but huge, and yellow, as morning glories never are. But is a squash plant in full flower more beautiful than one with both flowers and a half-dozen pattypan fruits perfectly ready to eat? A 'Red Sails' lettuce plant gone to seed (to flower, really, the stage before seed) is a magnificent plant. Tall, tapering to a peak, burgundy-and-green leaves smaller and smaller toward the top. And bitter, astringent to the tongue, oozing milky fluid. It is a lettuce plant in name only now, and well past the time when it can be considered edible. My palate-tempered vision of a perfect lettuce plant is of one that is not stately and regal, but rather frumpy and short. (In my earth garden, I have every once in a while left a lettuce plant that had bolted and was therefore no longer palatable. I had no urgent need for the space; and I did have a small but real desire to contemplate the plant in its own version of perfection. But in a container, space is precious, and I cannot indulge myself as much as I might had I the luxury of extra space.)

My first general rule for container-garden aesthetics is therefore that beauty is not in the eye of the beholder, but instead on the tongue. As is the case with most of my garden rules, I have no sooner made the rule than I begin to find ways to dodge it. My first dodge leads me to Rule Two: Unless there's a good reason not to, add some color to your garden. That's why I grow 'Bright Lights' chard instead of a garden-variety green Swiss chard. That's why I'm a sucker for lettuces that are other than all green.

'Bright Lights', for instance, appears in the earth garden every year, and it will appear somewhere in the container garden every year too. It is edible, and it is edible at many stages of maturity, but we don't really

◄ *Beauty and bounty. The edible blossoms of 'Scarlet Runner' beans also add visual spice to a vertical space.*

eat much of it. I'll go on growing it, and growing more of it than we'll eat, simply because it is stunningly beautiful and enjoyable to look at whenever I visit the garden. The same is true for many of the edible flowers we grow: their edibility gets them into the garden, but their beauty determines the extent of their presence. I always grow enough so that no matter how much we harvest, there's always some left to look at. The soul, too, needs sustenance.

Soul sustenance is the only excuse I can find for my other major rule-bender, chili peppers. Chili peppers are, according to some eaters, edible, but I don't eat them; nobody in my family eats them. But we use some container space for chili peppers every year, and we will to continue to do so. The plants in fruit are Christmas trees in July, and that's all they have to be to be part of my garden world. (Some of our friends do eat chili peppers, so we're able to give at least some of

▲ *Colorful chums. A container grouping of cilantro, 'Fairy Tale' eggplant, 'Red Robin' tomatoes with 'Freckles' and 'Red Sails' lettuce, and sage and dianthus offers a colorful, portable feast within easy reach.*

the harvest a home, and we keep a jar of dried peppers on the shelf over the spice rack . . . just for nice.)

Exceptions aside, most of what we grow in our edible container garden is there because we like to eat it, it is harvested when it is best to eat, and we grow as much of it as we will actually eat. Considerations of more-abstract beauty must operate most of the time within that culinary framework. But there is still a lot of room for beauty. A tasty salad may be the goal of my journey, but there are more and less scenic routes to that salad. There are actually colors, textures, and shapes galore for me to play with on the way to my meals.

Getting Beyond Green

At first look, it might seem that we're stuck with only one color on our garden palette — green. Later in the year we'll have some fruits, red, yellow, some purples, maybe orange. Along the way there will be some flowers as a prelude to those fruits, mostly flowers of yellow or white. But, it seems, for most of the time, most of the garden is green.

Subtle Shades

On second look, there's more to it than green, because there's more to green than first appears. To begin with, it's not really *green* we're talking about, but *greens*. 'Black Seeded Simpson' lettuce is green; so is 'Green Vision'; but they are very different greens, the former light and the latter full and dark. Even what is superficially the same shade of green will read differently on leaves of different textures. Now add a blush of red ('Red Cross' butterhead) or a spattering of red/maroon ('Freckles' romaine), and otherwise similar greens take on a new hue in a new context. We're not as limited as it might seem in our edible container gardens; we don't, it's true, have as full a range of colors to play with as there are in most flower gardens, but we have subtle variations in the range of colors that we do have. A lettuce garden can have all the beauty and mystery of a hosta garden or a rose garden or a stand of lilacs.

Blazing Colors

Some edible plants offer more than just subtle variations in color — they turn heads. Swiss chard comes in green, but also in red and yellow, and (like 'Bright Lights') as a multicolor mix of pink, gold, orange, red, purple, and white stems crowned with leaves that range from green to bronze. (By the way, if you start

'Bright Lights' seeds in a flat or tray and transplant the seedlings to containers, you can pick and choose the color accents you want.) Cauliflower comes in white, of course, but also in lime green, fluorescent orange, and an unbelievable purple.

Unexpected Color Combos

Later in the season, plants we grow for their fruits begin their contributions of color. You may think that tomatoes are red and violets are blue — but only if you know very little about either of them. Tomatoes are, indeed, red; but they are many shades of red, from pink to crimson, and they are also yellow, orange, brown ('Black Prince'), and green ('Striped Zebra'). And chili peppers! Greens, yellow, reds, orange, purple. Or try 'Numex Twilight' or 'Pretty in Purple', both of which start with purple and ripen through yellow, orange, and then red. All the colors can exist on the plant simultaneously. I grow a few chili peppers just because they help so much to make the container garden more exciting and colorful. We do, after all, have some color to play with, especially when we include edible flowers in our plan.

▼ *Dark roots. 'Purple Haze' is just one of the many colors of carrots you can grow, besides red, yellow, and (yes) orange.*

◀ *Veggies with pizzazz! Eating your greens can be colorful, too.* Clockwise from top left: *'Fairy Tale' eggplant, squash blossom, 'Lollo Rossa' lettuce with spicy bush basil and purslane, 'Wild Red' kale, a bed of mixed greens, and 'Bright Lights' chard.*

A Garden of Gardens

An earth garden can be groups of similar vegetables all growing together in a bed or a row, or things can be mixed up a bit, with different sorts of plants growing together in the same bed or row. The same goes for container gardens, although the rules governing what goes with what are different for containers. In the simplest container garden, single plants — a tomato or an artichoke, say — grow all alone, each in its own container. In a larger container, or with smaller plants, more than one plant may grow, but all the plants are of the same kind: all eggplants, all peppers, all lettuces. That sort of a garden doesn't take much planning. Just pick containers of a size appropriate to what's growing there, and arrange the containers so that all the edibles get the sun they need and everything fits together in a way that's pleasing to the eye.

▼ *Spicy stuff! 'Numex Twilight' peppers and spicy bush basil share space with a fledgling calendula in this self-watering copper cachepot.*

Mixing It Up

Variety is as nice a spice in the garden as it is in life. Why not grow some spinach in with the lettuce, or a pepper, an eggplant, and some celery in the same container? Why not a tomato with a broccoli plant or an artichoke? Or at least some basil and a few onions for a tomato sauce garden? Why not?

Based on the mistakes I've been able to make so far, some of these combinations will work just fine and others won't. The lettuces will grow well with the spinach — or any other salad green, for that matter. The pepper, eggplant, and celery will cohabit in peace as long as I give them a large enough container (40 quarts) to live in. But nobody's going to like living with a full-size tomato. The tomato will do just fine, but any plant trying to live in the same container will end up malnourished and stunted. The onions, with their puny little root systems, will barely grow at all. If you're going to try your hand at combining plants, choose dwarf varieties that will take up less soil space than their big brothers.

Therein lies the First Principle of Container Companion Planting: Group only plants of a similar mature size and with similar growth rates. Tomato plants grow to be big plants, and, once they get going, watch out! They will outgrow anything that tries to grow with them, and they'll end up with the lion's share of the food and water. The only companion that can successfully compete with a tomato is another tomato. The same is true of other large plants, like artichokes, squash, and corn, though they'll be a bit smaller than they would be if they didn't have to share the space.

One exception is to grow a plant that's harvested well before its companion matures. Early spinach, radishes, beet greens, or lettuces, for instance, can often be planted with squash, tomatoes, and other late-harvest vegetables. Lettuce seedlings will be long since eaten by the time those 'Eight-ball' zucchinis are harvested.

▲ *A taste of sunshine. Both the petals and the seeds of 'Big Smile' and 'Teddy Bear' sunflowers are edible. Instead of harvesting them, though, I usually leave the seeds for the chickadees.*

Although I've found that most vegetables grow best when they have the whole container to themselves, it can be fun to mix and match crops. The combinations on the following pages show plants that play nicely together and can stand a little competition for water and nutrients. Remember: the bigger your container, the more plants you can put in it!

ROBIN'S NEST

Most tomatoes are big bullies that will monopolize a container if given the chance. Not so with the dwarf cultivar 'Robin's Egg'(1); this is as big as it gets! It's perfectly happy to be nestled in among a bed of 'Red Sails'(2) and 'Freckles'(3) lettuce. Salads don't get any cuter than this.

(3) 'Freckles'

(2) 'Red Sails'

(1) 'Robin's Egg'

(3) 'Freckles'

(2) 'Red Sails'

(2) 'Red Sails'

(3) 'Freckles'

(2) basil

(3) parsley

(1) 'Bambino' eggplant

2

3   1

EGGPLANT PARMESAN

All the fixins! Most eggplants don't like to share quarters with other vegetables, but the dwarf cultivar 'Bambino'(1) grows well with one basil plant(2) and one parsley plant(3) tucked in next to it. The container is a large terra-cotta pot we converted into a self-watering container.

FALL FESTIVAL

When the air turns crisp and the tomatoes are finished, it's nice to know there will still be veggies to pick. We converted this cachepot into a self-watering container and planted it with 'Red Russian' kale(1), red cabbage(2), lemongrass(3), and a 'Chilly Chili' pepper(4).

(4) 'Chilly Chili' pepper

(2) red cabbage

(3) lemongrass

(1) 'Red Russian' kale

(1) calendulas

(3) 'Numex Twilight' peppers

(2) spicy bush basil

HOT AND SPICY

A mix for the Latin lover in us all. Yellow calendulas(1), spicy bush basil(2), and 'Numex Twilight' peppers(3) look and taste great together. They're also *muy simpatico* growing in this self-watering copper cachepot.

(1) red shiso

(3) mizuna

(4) arugula

(2) mustard greens

ASIAN FUSION

Who needs takeout when you've got all the ingredients for stir-fry on your back porch? We've planted up this stylish self-watering cachepot with red shiso(1), and a spicy mix of mustard greens(2), mizuna(3), and arugula(4). Turn on the rice cooker, but hold the wasabi.

HERBAL GALA

This container was designed for strawberries and works well for that purpose, but I like it even better as an herb garden. There's room for nine different herbs — in this case, sage(1), spicy bush basil(2), hyssop(3), thyme(4), and golden oregano(5), and in the back pockets of the container (not shown), chamomile, tarragon, marjoram, and rosemary.

(3) hyssop

(2) spicy bush basil

(1) sage

(4) thyme

(5) golden oregano

A TOUCH OF PROVENCE

Ooh la-la! Sage(1), thyme(2), fennel(3), and most other *herbes de Provence* are happy growing in a traditional container, so they can dry out from time to time. The medium-size pot is perfect for a small patio, where you'll have easy access to snip ingredients for your cassoulet.

(3) fennel

(2) thyme

(1) sage

(2) rosemary

(1) basil

(3) golden oregano

THE BOLD AND THE BEAUTIFUL

'Genovese' basil(1), rosemary(2), and golden oregano(3) look simply smashing together in this blue-glazed traditional pot. This combo would fare just as well in a medium-size self-watering container . . . perhaps at the beach house in Malibu?

REPLANT OFTEN

For a continuous harvest, the following veggies should be replanted every two to three weeks throughout the summer.

- arugula
- beets (when grown for greens and/or for baby beets)
- bush beans
- carrots (when grown for harvest when still young — just as the deep color develops)
- endive (when grown for baby greens)
- green garlic
- mâche
- mesclun greens
- mustard
- radishes
- spinach
- turnips (when grown for early harvest while still fairly small)

Keep on Truckin'

You'll get the most out of your container garden if all the containers are growing something all the time. For a large part of the garden, that's a given: tomatoes, peppers, corn, squash, cucumbers, and lots of other vegetables grow all summer long. But lettuce and spinach and other salad greens need only a part of the season to mature. Pole beans need a long season, but bush beans don't. Peas are done producing as soon as the hot weather arrives.

Succession Planting, Version One

Bush beans will go on producing beans as long as you keep picking all the beans that reach "eating stage" and don't let any of them mature to "seed stage," which is what the plant is trying to achieve. But as the harvest progresses, its quality declines; the later beans don't taste quite as good. (This is true only of bush beans, not pole beans.) To keep the bean harvest as its best, plant another container of bush beans two weeks after the first, and another about two weeks later. As the new crop begins to produce, pull the old plants, compost them, and sow a new crop of beans or something else in the container.

Lettuce mixes and the multi-greens salad mixes called mesclun can be harvested by cutting the plants ½ inch above the soil and then letting them grow again for another harvest. But the second harvest may not be as tasty as the first, and sometimes — especially in hot weather — some of the plants in the mix bolt and go to seed. Here, too, the way to ensure a top-quality harvest is succession planting, every week or ten days. Just take one cutting of the crop, then pull the plants by the roots and sow a new crop.

Succession Planting, Version Two

Some edibles grow and produce well at one time of the garden year but produce not as well — or not at all — at other times. Peas are done producing when hot weather arrives; lettuce seeds germinate well in cool weather, but not when it's hot. When the peas are done producing, plant some kale; the kale will be ready to harvest in the fall and on through the winter. As soon as any lettuce, arugula, or spinach plant heads for the salad bowl, put another (or the seeds for another) in its place. When the heat of summer puts an end to the lettuce harvest, plant some mini carrots for a late-fall harvest, or some claytonia for cool-weather salads. Check part three for other vegetables that prefer conditions at different parts of the growing season and therefore are good candidates for succession plantings.

◄ *Green window box. These greens are meant to be harvested young, cut-and-come-again. They are, therefore, planted densely, about an inch apart. We transplanted seedlings for the greens shown here, but they all could be started from seed in the container.*

▶ *Celery succession. Because celery is so shallow-rooted, it can be planted together with vegetables that grow down deep, like these beets. This is also a good way to plant in succession; the beets can be harvested early without disturbing the celery.*

CHAPTER EIGHT

CARING FOR YOUR CONTAINER GARDENS

Container gardeners have fewer chores than earth gardeners do, but the few we have are very important. We don't have to weed our gardens as much; we don't have to cultivate the soil; we spend less time than earth gardeners coping with diseases. But we do have to water, make sure our plants have enough food, and keep an eye out for pests.

Water Rules

Nothing of any consequence to a living plant happens in dry soil. Roots don't grow there. No nutrients pass from soil to plant. None of the symbiotic soil dwellers the plant needs live there. Dry soil isn't part of the plant's vital ecology. It just doesn't count. In a container, there is — compared with an earth-garden bed — very little soil. Every bit of that soil has to count, so as much of that soil as possible needs to be moist. That's the challenge of container gardening.

Watering Traditional Containers

Soil in traditional containers holds just the right amount of moisture only in the moments right after I have watered. Right after I have added all the water the container soil can hold, the moisture level is perfect. As soon as the plant or plants living in the soil begin to use some water, the soil holds progressively less and less water. As the amount of water in the soil drops, more and more of the soil becomes incapable of supporting plant life.

When I grow herbs in traditional containers, the water problem inherent in these containers isn't really a problem. I don't want those herbs to have optimum growing conditions all the time; I'm happy to introduce some stress into their lives so the herbs will taste better. But if I'm trying to grow vegetable plants, especially big ones like tomatoes, in traditional containers, I'll have to deal with the water problem.

In the balmy days of early summer, when the plants are still small, watering once a day may be enough. But in the dog days of summer, when the plants are large and demanding, watering may be necessary twice or three times a day . . . every day. And even that isn't really supplying plants with all the water they need for optimum growth. That's why I don't grow vegetables in traditional containers.

Self-Watering Containers

Plants in self-watering containers will always have enough water if the reservoir has some water in it. That's all there is to it. Make sure there's always water in the reservoir. Seems simple — but it's not. I need to know how quickly plants in any particular container are using up the water in that particular reservoir. Different plants use very different amounts of water, and plants use different amounts of water at different stages of their growth. Container reservoirs vary too, holding anywhere from a few pints to several gallons.

I check the water level in containers daily until I begin to get an idea of how much water the plants are using. After that, I'll begin to skip containers I'm sure will not need water, though I'll go back to more frequent checks if I notice any significant change in water use. (Plants use more water as they grow larger, and in hot or windy weather.)

◀ *Fill 'er up. The reservoir needn't always be full (and shouldn't be full just before a rainstorm), but it should contain some water all the time.*

By the time a plant wilts even a little bit, transpiration has been shut down and growth processes have stopped. To keep things going as well as we can in traditional containers, we need to water before plants suffer from lack of water. One way is to use a moisture meter to keep track of soil moisture at depths of about one and two inches. Observe the plants, and connect your observations with the soil moisture readings.

▲ *Watch it! Most self-watering containers have a gauge to help you see when the reservoir is getting low.*

The goal is to learn when to add water before any signs of stress appear. Alternatively, you can rely on your senses to determine when a plant should be watered. Does the soil look dry? If so, stick your finger down into it. Is the soil moist below the surface? If not, you'll know it's time to water, so you can reinvigorate the plant well before it starts to wilt.

THE GARDENER'S SHADOW

The time you spend watering and fertilizing offers you a good chance to get to know your plants better. It is while tending to your garden's water and food needs that you are most likely to discover any pest or disease damage requiring attention.

▲ *Time well spent. Whenever you water or fertilize your plants, take an extra minute to look for pests and other problems. Sylvia is checking the undersides of these eggplant leaves for aphids.*

You're never "just watering" or "just fertilizing"; you're paying attention to the plants, noticing changes in fruit production or leaf color, looking for potential problems. Not only does the plant benefit from this extra attention, but so do you; it makes watering seem like less of a chore!

HOW OFTEN TO WATER

How often you need to water depends on many things: on what you're growing and how much of it you're growing. On how old and, hence, how big the plants are. On how warm the air is, how windy, how humid. On how big the reservoir is.

The advertising blurbs for many so-called self-watering containers brag that you'll have to water only once a week, or even less frequently. To that I say, in a word, baloney. That might be the case if you're growing small flowering plants or slow-growing ornamentals, but most edibles are neither small nor slow-growing. They're big or, if they're small, you're probably growing many of them together. Large or small, they need to grow quickly, which means they'll need a lot of water, all the time. Mature tomato plants can go through a gallon of water a day. You'd need a container with a seven-gallon reservoir to hold enough water to satisfy that tomato plant for a week. Most containers have reservoirs with a capacity of two gallons or less.

In the context of vegetable gardening, the switch from traditional containers to self-watering containers does not necessarily mean that you won't have to water frequently; you won't have to water *as* frequently. And you'll be watering to keep the reservoir full, instead of coming to the aid of a plant that has suddenly found itself surrounded by parched soil. But you'll still have to water, and during the peak of the gardening season, you'll have to bring out the hose every day or two.

With a good self-watering container that has an adequate reservoir, and while plants are relatively small and undemanding, watering immature plants every other day or every third day will suffice, and seedlings may actually get by for a whole week. But many of my containers, even the ones with a large reservoir, need water daily in midsummer, and some, with smaller reservoirs and growing large plants like summer squash, may need water twice a day. The critical difference is that because they have a reservoir to depend on, the plants in self-watering containers are always getting the amount of water they need.

IN A DRY SPOT

Even though it doesn't have to be constantly filled to maximum capacity, there should always be some water in the container reservoir. If there is water down below, the wicking action of the soil will maintain moisture all the way to the soil surface.

If the soil surface ever becomes dry because the reservoir runs out of water, don't just fill the reservoir and expect things to proceed normally. The dry soil has lost its ability to wick moisture and needs to become wet again. Container soil, a large part of which is peat, actually resists water when it is dry; there won't be any capillary movement of water in dry soil. Peat needs to

▲ *Wetter isn't always better. Herbs like this lemongrass and variegated ginger mint taste better if they suffer through a little dry spell now and again; a bit of stress intensifies their flavor.*

be wet in order to get wet. Water from the top with a fine spray and keep watering until the soil is evenly moist and some water is draining into the reservoir. Then fill the reservoir.

There is an exception to this rule — if you're growing herbs in a self-watering container, you might want to let the reservoir go dry occasionally. They don't taste as good when they have an easy life.

SIGNS OF NUTRIENT DEFICIENCY

If the leaves of your plants are anything but dark green, chances are they need a boost of fertilizer. In many cases, you can tell which nutrients a plant is lacking by the color of its leaves. Since nitrogen is the key element in chlorophyll, a nitrogen deficiency becomes apparent when leaves turn yellow or light green. Red or purple leaves indicate phosphorus deficiency.

▲ *Help! Yellowing leaves are a sign of nitrogen deficiency.*

Other nutrient deficiencies are trickier to identify, but in general, slow growth and lack of vigor are usually good enough reasons to fertilize. You're after a full dinner plate, so it doesn't make sense to let plants limp through the season when you can give them the extra help they need to fulfill their harvest potential.

Well-Fed Veggies

My experience is that edible plants grown in a fortified, compost-based container mix like the ones described in chapter four may not need additional fertilizer during the growing season. But if you use different compost from the one I use, or if you use a container mix I haven't tried yet, you may not have the same results I've had. By the time a plant shows signs of nutrient deficiency (see box at left), some of the damage has already been done.

To be on the safe side, I would recommend supplemental fertilizing at six weeks after transplanting for long-season plants like artichokes, tomatoes, peppers, eggplants, and squash. I use a liquid fertilizer made from fish and seaweed. Fish/seaweed fertilizer supplies nitrogen, phosphorus, and potassium as well as many micronutrients and growth hormones. The amounts of N, P, and K vary with the brand, but are generally around 3-2-2 or 2-1-1. It does smell like fish and seaweed right after application, but the smell doesn't last very long. I add liquid fertilizer (mixed with water according to instructions on the package) to the container soil; you can also add it to the reservoir. I don't use granular fertilizer because I cannot work it into the soil without damaging the plant roots that grow just beneath the soil surface in the continually moist soil of a self-watering container. If you are growing edibles in traditional containers, you will definitely need to fertilize regularly (every other week for most plants; less frequently for herbs). Because traditional containers need to be watered from above, water-soluble nutrients are continually leached from the soil and carried out of the container with the water that exits the drainage hole in the bottom of the container.

A Little Snip Here . . .

Nature doesn't do pruning — not intentionally, at any rate. Pruning is not a way to help a plant grow the way it wants to grow; it's a way to get the plant to grow the way *we* want it to grow. Take a basil plant, for instance. Basil plants are quite happy to get on as quickly as possible with their life mission: grow just enough leaves to support the growth of some flowers at the end of each branch; see to it that the flowers are fertilized; make seeds. Mission accomplished. Faster is better because basil plants do not like cold weather and need to get all their life's work done in the heat of summer.

Enter Gardener. Gardener has a bit of a different agenda for basil. Gardener wants those leaves, not the flowers and certainly not the seeds. As soon as the flowers and seeds come into the picture, the plant's energy goes into making more flowers instead of more leaves, and the latter no longer taste the way Gardener wants them to taste. If I prune off all the tips of all the branches before the flowers appear, the frustrated plant responds by growing more branches and sub-branches and more leaves to grow on the branches to support some flowers . . . which Gardener again prevents by lopping off the terminal ends of the new branches. By and by, the basil plant becomes full and bushy with many tasty leaves and no flowers instead of being tall and lanky and covered with flowers and some bitter-tasting leaves.

▶ *Time for a trim.* I'm removing a sucker from this tomato plant so that it will develop a single main stem and be easier to train to a trellis.

There is something about a withered, pale yellow leaf that urges me to cut it off, to remove what I think of as a blemish. It looks ugly, but the plant is better off if I let that leaf fall in its own good time.

▲ *Not so fast! The yellowing leaves on this squash plant might be ugly, but they're serving a purpose. Let them be.*

Though pale and lacking in chlorophyll, and no longer able to help with photosynthesis and growth, it still contains stored nutrients that the plant can recycle and reuse. If a disused leaf or branch is obviously diseased, you can prune it off; otherwise, let it be until the plant is finished with it.

Control Your Plants!

Tomatoes, if they were in charge of how they were to grow, would not grow on trellises or tied to stakes; they'd crawl along the ground like the vines that they are. And tomatoes would not, on their own, limit themselves to one main stem; they'd send out side shoots all over the place, each of which would become a major stem. It's gardeners like us who want tomatoes to behave themselves and grow in a singular, stately, and upright manner, easy to tend and harvest. Tomatoes, the ones called "indeterminate," at least, have another preferred growth habit that operates at cross-purposes to a gardener's intentions. Tomatoes don't seem to notice that fall — and its attendant growth-ending frost — is coming. They'll go right on growing and growing and making new flowers, setting new fruits that have no chance to ripen before the season ends. So pruning is the way gardeners tame tomatoes and get them to behave as we think they ought to.

If grown in a cage trellis, tomatoes can be left to their own devices until later in the season. About a month before frost is expected, prune the growing tips of all the stems and remove any blossoms and small fruits that will not have time to mature and ripen. This way, a plant puts its energy into maturing fruits that have already set.

Growing tomatoes on a single trellis, on a stake, or on a cord suspended from a crossbar requires a more drastic style of pruning. Every sucker that appears on the main stem needs to be pruned off. Otherwise, each sucker becomes a new stem, and the tomato plant very quickly becomes impossible to trellis. When the plant grows to the top of the trellis, stop its growth by pruning the terminal shoot. The benefit to this method is that the plant does not become top-heavy and overwhelm its trellis.

Roping in the Strays

Some garden plants are by their nature upright and solid citizens; they have what is called a "compact growth habit." As long as you give them the space they need, they'll stay in that space and won't infringe on neighbors. But not all garden plants are like that; some have an urge to wander, and wander they will, taking over as much of the neighborhood as they can. Peas and pole beans, cucumbers, tomatoes . . . give them an inch and they'll take a yard. Wayward plants can make even a large earth garden with plenty of extra space into a jungle. Container gardeners don't have any space to spare; to grow these nomadic plants successfully in a container garden, we need to restrain and retrain their enthusiasm. Container-grown pole beans need to have some approximation of the poles they were named for; peas, even the short-vined varieties that the catalogs claim can be grown without support, grow better and are easier to pick when grown on a trellis. Cucumbers on a trellis grow straighter and are less likely to rot from being in contact with the soil. Tomatoes take up much less room grown on any sort of trellis, and their fruits are less likely to be eaten by slugs or snails.

Peas, cucumbers, and pole beans are designed for growing on a trellis; it's their natural habit to attach themselves to something. They'll climb netting or chicken wire or posts by reaching out and gripping with curly tendrils. Peas, and more often beans, do sometimes appear to get a bit confused; they send off stray tendrils away from rather than toward the support system. I gently redirect the erring sprouts; they usually get the point and attach themselves to the trellis. Sometimes, most often with peas, the mass of plant becomes too heavy and bulges out away from the trellis. I run a length or two of twine to support the plants and pull them closer to the trellis.

▲ *Wild vines. Indeterminate tomato plants need some support, like this metal cage, to keep them upright.*

SOMETHING TO HANG ON TO

If you can't attach a trellis to the container or drive supports into the ground, and if you don't have a nearby wall to attach a trellis to, rest the container on a couple of 2×4s or a piece of plywood. Attach the trellis supports to the wood base; the container weight will stabilize the whole structure.

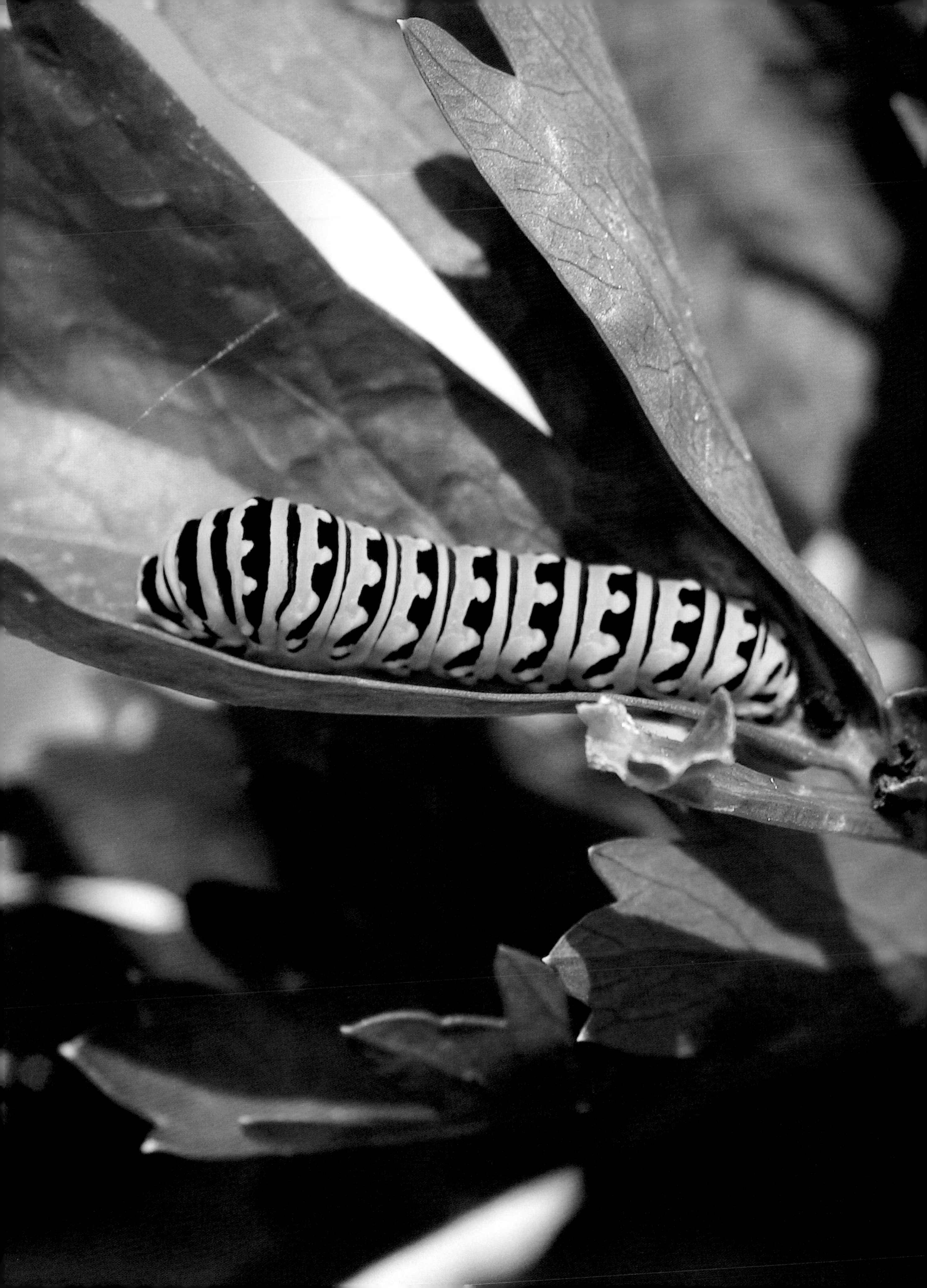

CHAPTER NINE

MANAGING PESTS AND DISEASES

The life of a gardener would be a lot simpler if gardeners were the only ones who enjoyed eating vegetables. But many other creatures — large, small, and very small — like to eat the fruits of our labor. Whatever their size or shape, garden pests are the bane of all gardeners.

Good News

There's good news right from the beginning: container gardeners will most likely have nowhere near the pest problems that most earth gardeners have in their gardens. A container garden on a balcony or a porch, or even a patio, is likely to be free of insect pests, because the latter are smart enough not to waste time looking for food in places where there has never been any.

Many of the plant diseases that plague earth gardeners from time to time — verticillium wilt, for instance — live in garden soil. The soils in container gardens have no garden soil; therefore, they are also free of soil-dwelling diseases. Other diseases, such as blossom end rot, are brought about by uneven watering, which won't be a problem if you use self-watering containers. A good compost, which makes up about half of the container soil I use, can help prevent all sorts of plant diseases. (If you do find something that might be a plant disease, refer to one of the references in the appendix.)

At various times in your gardening year, however, you *are* likely to find yourself competing with other creatures for the bounty of your garden's production. How can you make sure the competition between you and various garden pests is weighted in your favor and that most of your harvest ends up on your table instead of on the menu of some garden marauder?

Let's start by trying to avoid the problem altogether, or at least make it as small as we can. Then we'll identify ways to deal with whatever difficulties we can't avoid — ways that hopefully don't make things worse in the process of trying to make things better.

A garden pest is any creature feasting on what you're planning to feast on; in other words, it's something with the same taste in vegetables that you have. However, not all pest damage is significant enough to cause irreversible harm to a plant. Holes in the leaves of a mature tomato or bean plant — even quite numerous and substantial holes — usually bother the gardener a lot more than they bother the plant. In nature, there are always some insects nibbling on plants; that's just the way it is, and that's the way it has been for eons. Most of the time, what the insects eat is negligible; plants are designed to tolerate a certain level of damage. Plants in even the healthiest garden will have some insect damage, and they'll still produce a bountiful crop of mostly blemish-free food. Most of the time, the best advice for gardeners faced with small "pest" problems is "Don't just do something, stand there."

▲ *Gotcha!* Flea beetles have attacked much of this 'Red Russian' kale. Fortunately, a little damage won't drastically affect the growth of the plant.

The Rogues' Gallery

"Something" is eating little holes in the leaves of my cabbage transplants. "Something" ate all but the stem of a bean seedling last night. What should I do about that? First, let's find out what caused the problem. The pests you're about to meet are some (of the many!) that are *most likely* to cause problems in your garden.

Aphids

Aphids are the poster children for garden pests. Even if your garden is host to no other plant-munching creature, chances are you'll end up with some aphids. Look on the undersides of leaves, particularly young and tender leaves, and particularly the youngest and most tender leaves of young and tender plants.

Aphids are small, pear-shaped, and voracious. They come in various colors, but most of the aphids I've encountered are green, the better to blend in with their food. They feed by sucking the juices from leaves and stems; deformed and stunted leaves are a sign of aphid invasions. Just a few aphids won't harm a plant, but too many can kill it. Once they've settled in, aphids can increase their population from "just a few" to "too many" in a hurry, so it's best to deal with an aphid invasion as soon as it starts.

Control. The best defense is a good offense. If you can make the target plant distasteful or abhorrent to aphids, they'll look somewhere else for a meal. Hot pepper wax or garlic spray repels aphids. This works if the repellent is on the plant before the aphids arrive; in my experience, it doesn't drive them away if they're already there. Yellow sticky traps will capture aphids during their winged phase, when they are migrating to new plants.

In theory, at least, you can wash away the problem. Just the right amount of force in a spray of water directed at an aphid cluster will knock them off without hurting the plant. But that's a lot easier said than

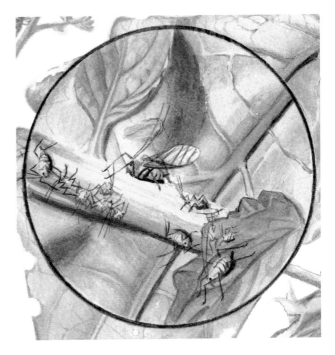

▲ *Green guys. Aphids can easily be spotted on the undersides of young leaves.*

done. The aphids, remember, are concentrated on the undersides of leaves, not the topsides, where they could be easy to spray off. And you have to hit every infested leaf and stem or the problem will quickly recur.

One possible solution is ladybugs; ladybugs love to eat aphids. And the mini alligator ladybug larvae *really* love to eat aphids. Purchasing and releasing ladybugs is a viable strategy for gardeners with big gardens and lots of aphids, but it's not likely to work for small container gardens. (When the ladybugs have eaten all the aphids, they fly away in search of more aphids in somebody else's garden and leave your plants defenseless again.) If I find ladybugs in places where they're not helping me — on plants other than the ones I'm growing, for instance — or crawling around on the house windows, I move them to aphid-infested plants. That strategy alone, however much it helps, rarely solves my aphid problems entirely.

▲ *Arachnophilia! Garden spiders prey on many kinds of insect pests, and should be grouped with the good guys.*

If all else fails, but only then, consider killing the little beasts. In order of potency — and, hence, collateral danger to other insects, good and bad — try insecticidal soap, neem, pyrethrum, or rotenone. The last two are quite potent and can harm even the gardener if carelessly used. Try to find a spray bottle whose nozzle can be turned upward, the better to spray leaf undersides. If there are many, many aphids on a plant or group of plants, I sometimes just pull the plants and dispose of them and the aphids. (Dip the plant in a bucket of soapy water to kill the aphids before you compost the plant.) It is sometimes better to cut your losses and just prevent the aphids from taking over the whole garden.

Flea Beetles

Flea beetles are right up there with aphids on my list of least-favorite garden visitors. They're the size of a pinhead, and dark brown or black; they look and behave like fleas. When approached, they jump, and quite a long distance. Then when you're looking the other way, they jump right back to the plant they were feasting upon. They eat little holes in leaves, especially the young and tender leaves of young plants. Flea beetles adore any member of the cabbage family (including oriental cabbages), the tomato family (including eggplant and pepper), and the beet family (including chard). A serious flea beetle attack can kill a young plant or stress it so much that it never amounts to much.

Control. Flea beetles like to hang around in weedy places, in piles of old leaves, in the detritus of organic waste that tends to accumulate around gardens. Flea beetles will be less likely to find your containers if those containers are not near the beetles' favorite haunts. Keep the containers away from weeds and organic waste. Containers located at least a couple of feet off the ground are both easier to tend and less welcoming to flea beetles.

Flea beetles (and other garden pests) can't eat what they can't get to. Group susceptible plants in containers and cover with a lightweight row cover like Reemay. The covers will have to be taken off any plant that needs to be pollinated, but by the time blossoms appear, the plant is usually tough enough that flea beetles are no longer interested. Plants like broccoli and cabbage that don't need pollination can grow under row covers all the time. It ain't pretty, but it works.

If you can't or don't prevent the problem, your only recourse is a botanical insecticide. I haven't found any repellent that deters these creatures.

Cabbage Worms

Cabbage worms are green, the better to hide on green plants, and about an inch long. There are also similar creatures, also green, called cabbage loopers. If it's an inch long and green and it's eating a cabbage or broccoli plant, it's a Bad Guy, and you'd be better off if it wasn't there. As pests go, these little caterpillars bother the gardener more than the garden: they usually don't do a lot of damage, but they're not much fun to find on your dinner plate. Because I often fail to follow the advice I'll give below, I spend extra time checking my broccoli (or soaking it in a saltwater bath) before I cook it, and I sometimes have to peel off a few worm-damaged outer leaves from the cabbage. In neither case is this a really big deal; I haven't lost the crop. Cabbage worms are one of the pest problems I sometimes just have to live with.

Control. If you do want to keep your brassicas worm-free, it's not really that difficult. The "worms" hatch from eggs laid on the plant by pretty white moths (gray, in the case of the cabbage looper). If a moth can't get to the plant to lay the eggs, there are no caterpillars to hatch from the eggs. One way to prevent the moth from laying eggs is to protect plants with a lightweight row cover. Cabbage worms are also prey to all sorts of predators like ladybugs, praying mantises, and trichogramma wasps; but none of them is going be much help with our half-dozen broccoli plants in containers. Handpicking is sometimes recommended, but I find it neither pleasant nor effective. (The "worms" are both difficult to grasp and quite soft, especially the small ones.) As a last resort, use Bt, but use it carefully because it can kill the caterpillar of any moth or butterfly, not just the targeted ones.

TOO MUCH OF A GOOD THING

Farmers or gardeners with very large gardens and serious aphid problems can purchase beneficial insects like lacewings, ladybugs, and praying mantises. That's not a viable option for container gardeners. The problem is that a large number of predators will quickly eat all the problem bugs in the small area and be left without any more to eat. If there's no more food, they'll have to move on to some other place, and eventually the "bad guys" return. When they do, there are no predators to control their numbers, and they can feed unmolested on their favorite garden plants — a so-called secondary outbreak.

▲ *Luck be a ladybug. Beneficial insects like praying mantises, lacewings, and ladybugs help keep gardens pest-free.*

Gardeners are best off having a resident population of predators large enough to eat most of the pests but small enough so they'll not eat *all* of them. If there's a healthy balance between pest and predator, the garden will survive. There will always be some damage, but never too much.

Colorado Potato Beetles

Even if you don't grow potatoes, you're likely to encounter this rascal. In a fairer world, this pest might well be called the Colorado eggplant beetle. Given its druthers, the Colorado potato beetle would eat eggplant leaves sooner than potato leaves. And it will, in a pinch, eat other members of this family — tomatoes and peppers included.

The adult beetles are quite attractive if I can for a moment ignore what they're doing in my garden — about a third of an inch long, with a black head, shaped like a large ladybug but with black and yellow stripes in place of polka dots. The children (larvae, to bug watchers) are, however, repulsive — plump, slimy, reddish blobs with legs. The eggs are bright orange and laid on the undersides of leaves. Adults and children alike eat holes in leaves. Enough of them can harm a plant, especially a young one. Fortunately, it is fairly easy to make sure that there are never enough of them to do much damage.

Control. Lightweight row covers would prevent the adults from getting to the leaves where they want to lay eggs. But row covers are not very pretty, and they also prevent bees and other pollinators from visiting eggplant, pepper, and tomato flowers, so I don't use row covers for these plants. The alternative? Handpicking. It's not that bad. The adults are easy to spot, grasp, and then drop into a can of soapy water. The larvae are a bit more of a challenge, but I can usually flick them off the leaves and into the water without actually grabbing hold of them. The most effective point of intervention with these creatures is the eggs. Whenever you find an adult beetle on a plant, search the underside of every leaf until you find some bright orange eggs. Then crush them. Or, if you find that too gross, clip off the leaf and dump it into the soapy water. (There is a Bt variety that kills the larvae, but I have never needed to use it, even on the potatoes in my earth garden.)

Cucumber Beetles

Small (⅓ inch) and narrow, the cucumber beetle comes in two versions, both with yellow wing covers but one with black stripes, the other with black spots. (They are known, respectively, as the striped cucumber beetle and the spotted cucumber beetle.) Although usually found on their namesake plants, cucumber beetles also feed on melons, squash, pumpkin, and occasionally beans and sweet corn. They also carry bacterial wilt, which can cause even more damage than their feeding.

Control. Row covers will prevent beetles from finding the plants in the first place. (Remove the covers for two hours in the morning twice a week after blossoms appear to allow pollination.) Use a handheld portable vacuum cleaner to suck up the beetles, and empty the vacuum immediately into a bag so the bugs don't crawl back out. Neem oil soap or pyrethrum will kill the beetles if it comes to that.

Earwigs

About ¾ inch long, brown, not very wide, and with formidable pincers on its tail end, the earwig is actually listed as a beneficial insect rather than a pest in many bug books. Earwigs prey on slow-moving, soft-bodied pests like aphids and the larvae of various insects; they also help break down the decaying organic matter they like to live in. That's the good news. Unfortunately, earwigs also have an appetite for young and tender garden plants; they can decimate the seedlings of beans, cabbage, celery, carrots, broccoli, and marigolds.

For longer than I like to admit, this fearsome-looking creature was the Mystery Marauder in our garden. Every morning, bean seedlings that had emerged the day before were defoliated, nothing left but the stems and the veins of what had been leaves. And the previous day's new carrot seedlings were gone. Nothing remained. There was no sign left behind to help me identify the culprit.

The damage obviously happened at night, so about midnight, flashlight in hand, I visited the garden and spotted an earwig scurrying down a bean stem and off into the darkness. None of my usually helpful bug books listed earwigs as a garden pest. An Internet search did unmask the perpetrator, however, and suggested a few ways to deal with the problem.

Control. If earwigs are becoming outlaws in my garden and eating my bean seedlings instead of the aphids I want them to eat, what do I do? Trap them, then kill them by dumping them into soapy water. How do I trap them? Earwigs are nocturnal: they forage at night and hide in moist, dark places during the day. To trap them, provide moist, dark places — moistened, rolled-up newspapers or sheets of cardboard laid on the ground are good options.

I was told I could place sections of bamboo near the damage zone in order to catch them. Uh-oh — the bean seedlings I've been telling you about? They were meant to grow on a trellis made of . . . bamboo. When I turned my bamboo bean trellis upside down and banged it on the inside of a plastic bucket, dozens of earwigs fell out. I had inadvertently created an Earwig Hilton right next to the Earwig McDonald's.

Earwigs will be less likely to plague container gardens that are off the ground, on benches a couple of feet high. If there are not very many earwigs about, let them be and hope they'll get most of their sustenance from aphids and the like. If they are too numerous and destructive, trap them — and don't use bamboo trellises in earwig country.

Tomato Hornworms

If I wanted to make a horror film about terrifying giant insects taking over the world, I'd give this creature the starring role. Tomato hornworms are large, green caterpillars, three to four inches long and as big around as your smallest finger. The "horn" is at the back end, sort of a spike-shaped tail. Tomato hornworms have an appetite to match their potential size and can devour a whole tomato plant in a couple of days.

Control. Inspect plants regularly to catch the problem while the caterpillars are still small. At that stage, spray with Bt or neem oil soap. The larger worms are easy to handpick and drop into a can of soapy water.

DON'T SHOOT YOURSELF IN THE FOOT

Many gardeners bring the curse of pests upon themselves by importing them on the leaves of plants they've purchased from garden centers or nurseries. Check purchased plants very carefully, especially the undersides of all the leaves, for signs of infestation. In the case of aphids, you'll notice clusters of the little green suckers fairly easily. Some insects, however, may be apparent only by the damage they've left behind. If you find evidence of pests on the plants you inspect, you may be better off buying your seedlings elsewhere.

ATTRACTING THE GOOD GUYS

You can attract predators to the garden by planting certain herbs and flowers or using commercially available attractants. Garden predators eat pests, but they don't eat just pests. They also eat pollen and nectar from certain plants. They'll move into your neighborhood and hang around if you provide them with their favorite flowering foods, some of which you might be growing as either edibles or ornamentals. Sweet clover, white alyssum, nasturtium, yarrow, fennel, dill, chervil, coriander, morning glory, and caraway are all on the Good Bug bill of fare.

▲ *Bring on the beneficials. Many ornamental edibles, like this nasturtium, provide pollen and nectar for predatory insects.*

Snails and Slugs

It's a bit of a shame, I feel, when a pretty bug plays the villain in my garden dramas. I don't like to have to terminate attractive creatures just because they're interfering with my plans to bring food to the table. I do it, but I don't like doing it. But slugs are altogether another story; I have no ambivalent feelings here. Slugs look just as horrid as they act. They're slimy, homely, and utterly without socially redeeming qualities. They'll eat just about anything in the garden they can get to, leaving behind a slimy trail to let you know who's responsible for the carnage.

Control. Slugs and snails (slugs wealthy enough to own a mobile home), in order to maintain their moist and slimy nature, seek out dark and damp places; they work at night or under cover. Like vampires, they avoid the light and heat of the sun. Because they move slowly, slugs and snails are easy to catch . . . provided you can find them. Go hunting at night with a flashlight or set up some traps — boards or stones laid on the ground that the critters can hide under. Slugs are not much fun to grab, but they can be shoveled up on the end of a popsicle stick or something similar. However you do it, get them into a can of soapy or salty water. You can also kill them in place by sprinkling them with a little salt or wood ashes.

I find it more pleasant to try to avoid slug encounters altogether. Put containers on benches rather than on the ground. Thirty inches is a few small steps for a gardener but a heck of a hike for a snail or a slug. Put a band of copper foil around the bench legs; slugs evidently get a shock crossing copper and therefore avoid it. You can slug-proof containers on the ground by plugging drainage, overflow, or fill holes with a piece of a copper scouring pad. Surround the container area with a band of wood ashes, dry sawdust, diatomaceous earth, or crushed eggshells. A saucer of stale beer attracts slugs; they crawl right in and drown.

The Good Guys

I have a tendency I should guard against when it comes to insects: whenever I see a bug, particularly an ugly one, on one of my garden plants, I assume the worst. That bug is obviously there to eat *my* food. Of course, that's not the only possibility. The bug could be there to eat the bugs that are eating my food. And in fact that is often the case. There's always a lot of eating going on in nature; where there is a bug eating a plant, there will soon be a bug or other creature eating the plant-eating bug. It is, therefore, much to my advantage if I am able to identify the "good guys" so that I do not mistakenly kill off my allies.

Ladybugs

Ladybugs, a.k.a. lady beetles, are right up there with chickadees on my list of favorite creatures. They are cute, and I'm a sucker for cute. But ladybugs are more than that, and they earn all the good vibes I send their way. Ladybugs eat aphids; any bug that eats aphids is a gardener's friend. They also eat mealybugs, mites, thrips, the larvae of Colorado potato beetles, and other soft-bodied insects — around 5,000 plant-munching pests per ladybug lifetime. Most people with whom I've discussed ladybugs recognize them and have some idea that they're helpful, or at least not harmful. Almost none of those people recognize ladybug larvae. Ladybug larvae, unfortunately, are as ugly as their parents are cute. They're oval, dark brown with orange spots, and covered with bristles. They, like their parents, eat aphids and the like. Learn to recognize this homely gardener's friend and protect it whenever you see it.

Praying Mantis

Often considered a poster child for beneficial insects, the mantis is, in spite of its size and ferocious appearance, not as helpful in the garden as a bunch of ladybugs or green lacewing larvae. Still, they do eat pests (though they'll also eat beneficials and pollinators if they can catch them) and they're fun to watch.

There are other beneficials, though none as obvious and colorful as these. If you see strange bugs on your plants that are not obviously eating the plants, they might be searching out pests. Check a good book to confirm the identity of any suspected pest before making any effort to eliminate it.

Green Lacewing

This delicate creature doesn't look like much of a pest killer. And it isn't, at least not in its adult phase. But when the green lacewing slips into a handy phone booth and changes into its Superbug larval phase, watch out, all you aphids and thrips, spider mites and mealybugs, all you soft-bodied plant munchers. The Aphid Lion is on the loose! Green lacewing adults also feed upon the nectar of certain flowers. (See "Attracting the Good Guys," page 110.)

- **Use barriers** (fabric row covers, repellents, odiferous companion plantings) to prevent contact between pest and host.
- **Use traps** to lure away pests from target vegetable plants.
- **Handpick troublesome pests.** A 15-minute early-morning tour of the garden is all it takes to keep Colorado potato beetles under control by handpicking.

- **Use benign and selective controls,** such as insecticidal soap.
- **Use botanical insecticides only as a last resort,** after carefully considering the consequences.

Don't Go Nuclear

As I said before, the goal is not to kill *all* the pests. The goal is to kill *some* of the pests, just enough so that the damage they do is not significant. This paradox is at the heart of the ecological approach to pest management. In the ecologically healthy garden, the natural predators of various pests usually keep the number of those pests low enough so that the damage they do does not interfere with the growth of your plants and the usefulness of their product. If this is to happen, there must be some pests available all the time for the predators to eat. Otherwise, the predators will either starve to death or move away to an environment that contains enough food . . . like somebody else's garden. The problem here is the same as it is in the rest of nature: predator populations lag behind prey populations. Compared to their predators, garden pests produce more young, do it more often, and mature more quickly. When all the predators of a pest are gone and the pest returns, it can very quickly establish a large and significantly destructive population before being confronted again with predation, in what is called a secondary outbreak (see "Too Much of a Good Thing," page 107).

Organic Insect-Pest Control Methods

An ecologically sound pest-fighting strategy involves using the least disruptive methods we can, moving on to less benign methods only when we have to. Start with ways you can prevent pest problems; then move on to ways you can solve whatever problems you couldn't avoid.

Plants are much more vulnerable when they are young. The same number of pests on a young, small plant and a large, mature plant will defoliate the first and barely upset the second. Tender, easy-to-eat plants are more attractive to pests than are older and tougher ones. Our pest strategy for young plants needs to include careful monitoring, because the pests are more likely to be on young plants than elsewhere. And we

GOTCHA COVERED

The quick and easy way to keep pests from plants is to cover the plants with a lightweight row cover. (The good news is that many pests are pesty for only a short time, so some of the covers can come off after the danger is past.) Lightweight row covers are light enough to drape directly on plants, but I prefer to have some distance between the fabric and the plants, so I use wire hoops* to support the covers.

1 Drill a hole in the container lip at each corner. The wire should be a very snug fit in the holes.

2 Wiggle the ends of two sturdy wire hoops into the holes.

3 Where the wires cross, fasten with a length of wire.

4 Drape and fasten a piece of row cover, using a bungee cord and a length of rope.

5 The bungee cord enables you to remove the row cover more easily than if you just used rope.

* The hoops I use are sold by many gardening-supply companies, and are normally used for supporting woven row covers in the earth garden.

have to deal with pests sooner and at lower population levels because young plants cannot tolerate damage as well as older plants can.

MIX THINGS UP

As a general rule, diversity is a good idea in nature and in gardens, whether in the earth or in containers. A diverse ecology including many different sorts of plants supports a diverse ecology both above and below the soil. There are pests feeding on plants, but there are also predators feeding on the pests. And there is a full complement of creatures large and small that help plants grow — bees and butterflies and beneficial fungi and bacteria. In an earth garden, we'd work toward biological diversity by interplanting or companion planting, growing different plants in close proximity,

▲ *Let me be. Many of the pesticides gardeners use in the war on pests also kill beneficial insects and butterflies. If you want monarchs and swallowtails in your garden, leave the spray on the shelf.*

in the same bed or row. In containers it's not generally a good idea to mix plants with different needs in the same container. But container gardeners can still mix things up by setting pots of different plants together in one spot. Unless there's only one sunny place available, there's no need to group all the containers of tomato plants together. Pair a tomato with an artichoke or a container of onions, broccoli, or kale. Put the salad-garden container near the onions or the beets. Place a few pots of dill and fennel around them, to attract beneficial insects.

KEEP ONE STEP AHEAD OF TROUBLE

In our earth garden, we try to avoid pests and diseases that winter over in the soil by moving things around every year, rotating crops to a different place in the garden. In our container garden, we have a similar rule: Don't plant tomatoes (or a crop from the same family — in this case, peppers or eggplant) in the same container two years in a row. We often dump containers at the end of the season, wash them out, and refresh and remix container soil for a new garden year. In this case, we may use the same container for the same plants. (To be on the safe side, disinfect all containers each year with a solution of 1 part bleach to 10 parts water.)

There's No Such Thing as a Pesticide

Most of what we are taught to think of as pesticides are in fact much more than that. They are insecticides, in that they are often capable of killing many more kinds of insects than just those listed on the label as target species. Among the insects that may also be harmed are pollinators and those that prey upon the pests.

Even a relatively carefully aimed killer like Bt, a bacterium used to control various pests on cabbage, corn, and tomato plants, isn't totally without "collateral damage." Although the target is supposed to be the caterpillars that munch on plants of the cabbage family or the ones that eat tomato leaves or corn kernels, any caterpillar that ingests some Bt-infested food will die from it. If some Bt gets on a carrot or parsley plant where the caterpillar that will become a black swallowtail butterfly is feeding, that potential butterfly will die. Or if some Bt ends up by accident on a milkweed plant, the monarch butterfly larvae feeding there will die. The bacterium is just as deadly to those kinds of caterpillars as it is to the little green ones we sometimes find in our broccoli.

"NATURAL" DOES NOT MEAN "HARMLESS"

Just because something called a pesticide is derived from natural sources or approved for organic production does not mean that it is a good idea to use it in your garden. True, poisons derived from plants — like neem (extracted from the seed of the tropical neem tree), pyrethrins (from a daisylike chrysanthemum native to Kenya), and rotenone (from a tropical plant of the genus *Derris*) — are less dangerous than chemical pesticides because they break down quickly and therefore do not build up in the food chain or remain active in the soil.

But these are poisons nonetheless, and quite potent ones in the cases of pyrethrin and rotenone. They do affect beneficial insects and beneficial microbes. They can, by killing too many of the target insects, lead to a depletion of natural predators and bring about secondary outbreaks of pests. Use them with care and only when all other efforts have failed.

* Kills Aphids, Mealybugs, Mites, Whiteflies
and other listed pests.
See Back Panel
* For Indoor & Outdoor Uses

ACTIVE INGREDIENT........... BY WT
Potassium Salts of Fatty Acids....... 2.00%
OTHER INGREDIENTS............ 98.00%
TOTAL............ 100.00%
KEEP OUT OF REACH OF CHILDREN
See back panel for additional
Precautionary Statements and First Aid.

Insect
Killing S
WITH SEA
EXT

Big Pests

Most of the damage in gardens is done by little pests, like insects. Because little creatures can't eat very much, it takes a large number of small pests working for a while to cause significant damage. But one big pest can ruin a whole season's work in just one night. One deer in one night can eat all of my pea crop and most of the vines they're growing on. One woodchuck can do in all my broccoli seedlings. One raccoon can destroy my whole corn patch. (Wild pests aren't the only culprits in this category — our dog, Coal, eats peas, raspberries, corn, and tomatoes when he gets the chance. A cat mistaking your container garden for a litter box can make a big mess without eating anything.)

Deer

When I grew up in semirural Connecticut, deer were unheard of; I didn't see my first deer until I was a teenager on vacation in northern Maine. Now deer are pests in suburban gardens all over the country. If your containers are on a balcony or a rooftop, you won't have a problem. But if deer munch on the earth gardens or landscape plants in your neighborhood, chances are they'll take a shine to your container garden, too. This is especially true during times of drought, when natural sources of food for deer are not readily available, and they'll be especially happy to graze if you plant their favorite foods — which is pretty much everything we like to eat. The one thing deer are unlikely to eat is pungent herbs; the strong scent and flavor actually seem to act as a deterrent.

Raccoons and Other Critters

I made the mistake last year of assuming that raccoons wouldn't bother with container-grown corn. (No, I cannot explain why I assumed that.) I fenced the earth garden corn but not the container corn, and a raccoon ate all the container corn the night before we were planning to harvest it. The earth garden corn was untouched.

Although squirrels and skunks may also partake of your edibles, sometimes they damage container gardens just by digging. Freshly transplanted seedlings and rows of seeds can be upset or tossed out onto the deck by a squirrel looking to bury his cache of nuts. In cities, where there is a plethora of squirrels and not a lot of soil, a container can become a prime burying ground. Cats can also do a lot of damage by digging.

Controls

Many garden centers and catalogs feature repellents that, they claim, keep away deer and other animals. These include all manner of sprays and powders, from garlic and eggs to blood meal and human hair. Some are scent-based deterrents; some are taste based. (The animal has to actually bite into the deterrent-covered plant to know that he doesn't want to eat it — not ideal when you're growing edibles!) Keep in mind that many repellents are not meant to be used on edibles. If you choose to use a repellent, make sure you select one that is safe for use on food crops.

◄ *A harvest helper. Our dog, Coal, sometimes gets to the tomatoes (and peas and strawberries) before we do!*

The Fence: Your Best Defense

For many years our earth garden has been free of deer, and our corn patch free of raccoons, thanks to electric fencing. I string one wire (it's actually a plastic cord interwoven with tiny metal wires) at about deer-nose height (about three feet) all the way around the garden.

Even if you'd prefer an electric fence, that might not be an option in your neighborhood. Also, you may not want to string electric fencing around your entire deck if you're planting only a container or two. A four-foot-high fence of chicken wire or plastic mesh will be enough to deter smaller creatures, but it won't keep out deer. Another option is to cover the target containers with chicken wire formed over the frame described in chapter five for use with row covers.

▲ *Zzzzap! A simple electric fence may be all you need to keep raccoons and deer out of your garden. Although most systems sold for home use don't deliver a jolt of dangerous voltage, you'll likely want to post a sign to let visitors know the fence is turned on.*

CHAPTER TEN

HARVESTING THE BOUNTY

Now comes the really fun part — the harvest! Starting with the first radish and ending with the final tomato ripening on the windowsill, the joys of eating join the pleasures of tending plants. But whether you get all of your reward or only part of it depends on how and when you harvest, and on whether the veggies you pick are ripe. Knowing when to harvest is the key to getting the most out of your edibles.

Is It Ripe Yet?

From the plant's point of view, *ripe* means that the plant has reached maturity and attained the goal of its life: reproduction. Most plants have a mission to produce mature seeds.

To a gardener, *ripe* means that whatever part of the plant we intend to eat is at its peak of flavor and/or nutrition, or at the stage where it will store best for future eating. Sometimes what is ripe for the plant is also ripe for the gardener. Sometimes, from the gardener's perspective, there is more than one stage of ripeness, only one of which is also ripe as far as the plant is concerned. And sometimes — quite frequently, really — the plant's notion of ripe is very different from the gardener's.

▼ *Ripe and ready.* Clockwise from top left: *Picking green beans at the right stage of ripeness can be a tricky business. Most tomatoes ripen slowly from green to red. Unlike other varieties, this white cucumber doesn't indicate ripeness by turning dark green. These red bell peppers look about ready.*

Looking for Maturity

A tomato is at its peak of flavor when it contains mature seeds. If properly saved and sown in the spring, the seeds of a ripe tomato will germinate and produce a tomato plant. The same is true for melons, pumpkins, and winter squash. How can I tell, without actually examining the seeds, when it is time to harvest this sort of edible?

This is more art than science. After a while, you'll correctly identify fruits that "just look ripe," and you may or may not be able to explain the reasons for your choices. I think I know why I harvest what and when I do, but I'm not entirely sure that I'm aware of everything that goes into the decisions.

A RIPE COLOR

After a while of looking and tasting, the subtle differences between a tomato that is just red and one that is red-ripe become apparent. Different varieties may have somewhat different reds, or even different colors, but there is a color for every variety that says, "This fruit is really ripe."

Often the most important color on a ripe fruit is the one that isn't there — green. All the fruits we're considering here start out green, and as long as they stay green or partially green, they're not yet ripe. The exceptions to this rule are some greenish melons and squashes, and tomatoes like 'Green Zebra' that actually ripen green; but even fruits that ripen green ripen to a different hue than when they were immature.

BREAKING THE BOND

A surer sign — one to check if the color seems to be right — is some indication that the bond between plant and fruit has begun to weaken. On a really ripe tomato, the little bonnet of leaves right where a tomato attaches to its stem and the stem itself are withered; the tomato will separate easily from the plant if lifted gently.

THE SUPERMARKET STANDARD OF RIPENESS

If your standard of *ripe* is based on what you're used to seeing in the produce section of the supermarket, you may be missing the best of your garden by harvesting too soon or too late. Food merchants have to be more concerned with how well a product ships over long distances and what its shelf life will be than with how it tastes.

▲ *For the love of squash! Pattypan squash is best when picked young.*

Some vegetables — tomatoes and melons, for example — are picked by growers too early, before they are fully ripe and sweet. They can, and usually do, continue to ripen after harvest, but they never achieve the flavor they would have had if they had matured on the vine. Most of us judge ripeness by what we've seen at the market. But once you've tasted a pattypan squash picked while it is small (two to three inches) and tender and sautéed lightly within minutes of picking, you'll start to develop a whole new set of standards.

A Young and Tender Harvest

For many of the other plants we grow in the edible garden, the proper harvesttime for the gardener is sometimes quite different from the plant's idea of maturity.

Pea plants, for instance, are mature when they've produced big, dry, wrinkled, utterly tasteless seeds — the sort of unappetizing objects that come in a packet of pea seeds. That's a far cry from the gardener's goal of small, sugary, moist, tender, bright green, and delicious peas that go so well with new potatoes and a bit of butter and salt. The gardener's idea of a ripe pea occurs in a short stage in the plant's life cycle, when the potential pea seed has the most sugar it will ever have,

just before the plant starts turning the sugar to starch to ensure a long storage life into the coming spring.

When a plant is best harvested at its maturity, the gardener needs to look for a plant's stage of lowered vitality and gradual decline. When, as in the case of peas, a plant's idea of ripe is not the same as ours, we need to figure out another way to know when it is time to harvest.

▲ *Not ripe yet. Peas are one vegetable that should be picked on the young side, but these pods are still a few days away from harvest size.*

Looking for Tenderness

Harvesting is a somewhat intuitive process of observing and gathering information about the plant, making a choice, acting on the choice, evaluating the results, and then trying again. To get the best harvest of peas, for example, you have to train your eye and hand to predict what is inside the pod from what you see and feel outside the pod: a subtle combination of size, plumpness, and color. Choose a pod that "looks right," and give it a gentle squeeze to get a feel for what is inside; then open the pod and taste the peas. How close was your guess to the reality? Try again until you're consistently picking pods with good-size peas at the peak of sweetness. Because taste is a matter of preference, only you can decide what is "ripe enough" for harvest.

Making the Harvest Last

Harvesting young, before the seeds have developed much, also works well for summer squashes, eggplant, and pole beans, all of which taste best when picked long before their seeds have reached maturity. You can also extend the harvesttime for bush beans (both green and yellow) this way, but the beans from the later part of the harvest won't taste quite as good. To get the best taste from bush beans over a longer period of time, try a series of small succession plantings every week or so. Harvest from a planting for a week or 10 days; then cut or pull up the plants, add them to the compost bin, and start picking from the next planting.

Check plants at least every other day, and pick all the fruits of the right size. If any fruits manage to escape and grow too large, pick them and compost them so the harvest can continue. Otherwise, the plant will begin to decline.

▶ *Dinnertime! Nothing beats a bowl of freshly picked green beans.*

HOW TO PICK PEAS AND BEANS

There's a "when" to pick peas and beans. There's also a "how." You might be tempted to pick pea pods one-handed, sort of yanking them off the vine. That'll work sometimes. Other times, though, you'll find yourself pulling a section of pea vine off the trellis, because the pea pod didn't separate easily from the vine. Picking peas and beans is really a two-handed operation — one to hold the vine right where the pod attaches, one to pull on the pod. It's slower that way, but you'll do less damage to the plant. By continuously harvesting peas and beans, you'll also make the plants more productive. Once they start to set mature pods with fully ripened seeds, the plants will stop producing new pods. So remember: Pick well, and pick often!

Picking Leaves

A lot of what we grow in the edible garden is grown for its fruit; we may choose to harvest that fruit and the seeds it contains quite a bit before it is fully mature, but it is the fruit and seeds we are after. What we usually call leaf vegetables present a completely different harvest conundrum. The right time for harvest here is a long, long way from the biological end point of the plant's life. We harvest lettuce and spinach, for instance, so long before maturity that many gardeners have never seen a mature lettuce plant — as it looks first in flower, then in seed. Gardeners want the leaves from a lettuce plant, but for the plant, those leaves are but the means to an end. Lettuce plants want just as badly as any other plant to produce a crop of seeds. The leaves are there to make possible the great amount of photosynthesis that a substantial stalk and bountiful flowers and seeds will require.

The "proper" time to harvest leaf vegetables is very much a matter of personal preference. Leaves tend to be more tender but have a milder taste when they are young and little, what many markets now call "baby greens." If that's the way you like your greens, harvest when the plants are about three weeks old and the leaves are two to three inches long; clip them with scissors about a ½ inch above the soil line. The plants will regrow once, sometimes twice. Keep a full salad bowl by planting a new crop every two weeks. (If you plan to harvest this way, plant very densely.)

If your tastes run to stronger flavors, space plants farther apart (see part three) and plan on waiting until the leaves are four to six inches long. Either harvest the outer leaves and let the center leaves get larger or harvest the whole plant.

▼ *Take your pick. Mizuna can be either sheared with scissors or picked one leaf at a time.*

THREE WAYS TO HARVEST GREENS

Depending on what kind of leafy greens you're growing and how long you want the plants to last, you can pick a salad three different ways:

Cut-and-come-again. Hold a cluster of leaves with one hand. Cut them about ½ inch above the soil level with scissors.

Try with:

- mesclun mix (pictured)
- any densely planted greens

One leaf at a time. Cradle a leaf in your fingers and pinch it from the plant with your thumbnail.

Try with:

- spinach (pictured)
- leaf lettuces
- any sparsely planted greens

Off with its head. Cut the stem at soil level with a sharp knife.

Try with:

- head or loose-leaf lettuce (pictured)
- cabbage

The Snackable Bouquet

Unlike many other edibles, judging ripeness in flowers is easy: they're "ripe" when they're in bloom. In most cases, we're using edible flowers as a festive garnish or to add a little zip to salads (many flowers are quite spicy), so we usually pick only as much as we need for a meal.

Whether you're picking the individual petals of a sunflower or snipping the whole blossoms of chives, violas, basil, nasturtiums or claytonia, the time of day makes a difference. Harvest flowers in the morning, after the dew has dried but before the heat of day, or in the evening, before the dew settles. Use immediately or refrigerate for a day or so, wrapped loosely in a damp paper towel in a plastic bag.

Eats Shoots and Flowers

When I think of "edible flowers," I generally think of flowers that are the only edible product of the plant in question. But squash blossoms are edible; so are pea and bean blossoms. Tender pea shoots stir-fried

with garlic are a seasonal specialty in Asian cuisine. Of course, if I develop too much of an appetite for pea shoots or squash flowers, I'm going to cut into my harvest of peas and squash. In addition to having edible leaves, chives produce flowers that make a colorful and tasty garnish for a salad. Claytonia flowers can be eaten right along with the leaves that cradle them, as can basil flowers. Check the herb section of part three for other edible flowers where you'd least expect them.

Artichokes and broccoli are, in a sense, edible flowers. More accurately, they're edible flower buds. They're at their edible best in the bud stage and become overripe as soon as the flowering process begins. The petals of an artichoke bud begin to separate as the bud starts to open. Broccoli heads — really a huge cluster of tiny flower buds — lose their tight form and begin to turn a bit yellow. These edible flowers, at the flower stage, are no longer edible.

Here are some of the many edible flowers:

- bachelor's buttons
- borage
- calendulas
- chamomile
- chives
- dianthus
- gem marigolds
- nasturtiums
- sunflowers
- violas

◀ *More than good looks. Make dinner more colorful by adding a few edible flowers. Clockwise from top left: Violas, marigolds, broccoli (technically a flower bud), borage, nasturtiums, and garlic chives.*

PICKING PEPPERS

The vegetable we commonly call a green pepper is green when we eat it only because we harvest it when it is, in the context of its life cycle, unripe. The seeds in a green pepper are not yet mature and cannot reproduce. If we left the green pepper longer on the plant, it would turn red (or yellow, lavender, or even chocolate brown, depending on the variety). The seeds would be mature and produce pepper plants if saved and preserved properly. The taste would change too, becoming sweeter and milder.

Harvesting peppers while they are unripe interrupts the pepper plant's life cycle and changes not only the product of the harvest but also its size. When a pepper plant has succeeded in producing ripe (red, yellow, whatever) peppers full of mature seeds, its life mission is accomplished and its life is over. It will stop blooming and setting fruit and go into decline. If, however, we keep harvesting peppers while they are green, the pepper plant will continue, as long as weather conditions allow, to put forth blossoms, set fruit, and try to mature that fruit to the "proper" stage. You'll end up with a bigger pepper crop if your standard of ripeness is "green."

CHAPTER ELEVEN

WHEN WINTER DRAWS NEAR

The days are getting shorter and shorter and the nights are cooler now; there's a hint of frost in the evening air tonight. There are still a few vegetables left to harvest, but it's time to start the bittersweet process of bringing down the curtain on this year's Garden Show.

Extending the Season

According to the weather report, the first fall frost will happen tonight. Is there anything we can do to keep our gardens going a bit longer? Yes. Container gardeners can do the same things that earth gardeners can do, and we also have a few options they don't have.

The Great Cover-Up

Container gardeners and earth gardeners can mitigate the effects of freezing temperatures by covering plants with woven fabrics called *row covers*. Medium-weight covers will protect against two or three degrees of frost; heavier-weight fabrics, four to six degrees. Not all garden plants need this sort of help, but many do. Tomatoes, peppers, and eggplants; squashes, melons, and beans — the heat lovers of summer are the frost fearers of fall. (Basil, the garden wimp, is very sensitive to frost and may not survive even with help. We harvest all of our basil before the first frost.) Celery can tolerate a degree or two of frost, but I usually cover it anyway, just in case the temperature drops more than predicted.

Although the covers will work just sitting lightly on the plants, the leaves in contact with the cover will sometimes become frosted, so I prefer to drape the row covers over frames of heavy-gauge wire attached to the containers, as shown at left. (Instructions for making the frame are in chapter five.) In a pinch, old sheets, towels, or tarpaulins will serve. If plants do get frosted, spray them with water first thing in the morning, before the sun has melted the frost.

▲ *Covering lunch. When frost threatens, you can keep plants from freezing by draping them with a piece of row cover or simply a bedsheet.*

A Moving Experience

There comes a time in every gardening year when covers won't do the trick any longer. When the killing frost finally arrives, that's the end of the poetry reading for earth gardeners. But it doesn't have to be the final act for container gardeners.

If the containers are not too heavy — or if you can round up some help — move the plants to shelter rather than moving shelter to the plants. Earth gardeners can't do this, but container gardeners can move plants indoors when cold temperatures are forecast. Even an unheated garage or shed will protect against quite a few degrees of frost. If you have your containers on wheeled dollies, you can move them to a shed, garage, or closed porch where they'll be able to wait out the cold, then put them back outdoors when the weather improves.

Sylvia and I always plan to move some containers indoors as soon as the cold weather arrives. We make a small garden right in the kitchen — small pots with herbs, a window box salad garden planted in the fall for a winter indoor harvest, a cherry tomato started late in the spring to begin producing in the fall, a celery plant for soups and snacks. If the plants are mature when we move them inside, they don't need much light; they're not, after all, going to be growing much more. The goal is not to *grow* the plants, but to *preserve* them in good shape for a few weeks while we harvest them. It is possible to keep this sort of garden, with plants in a state of suspended animation, well into the winter, but because there is very little natural light available at that time of the year, it is not usually feasible to grow plants from seed. The growing season starts up again with the longer days of spring.

WON'T THEY FREEZE?

Some edibles can survive a bit of frost (celery, for example), and some can take a bit more (most lettuces, broccoli, cabbage, and chard), but some actually relish it. Spinach, kale, and a few lettuce varieties have evolved a cold-weather strategy that allows them to survive even subzero temperatures with ease. As colder and colder temperatures signal the coming of winter, these plants begin to produce compounds (including sucrose) that act as antifreeze; they prevent the formation of ice crystals within a plant's cells.

By the time really cold weather arrives, spinach, mâche, and kale are ready to survive whatever Mother Nature serves up. As an unintended culinary bonus, these "chilled-out" salad greens are sweeter than they were before the frost hit them. We have found a few lettuces ('Winter Density', 'Rouge d'Hiver', 'North Pole', and 'Arctic King') that will survive very cold weather, though they are not as hardy as spinach and kale, which we have seen survive at –25°F (–31°C).

Last-Minute Harvest

Sooner or later, even for container gardeners, it's time to call a halt to most of the garden. But even then, all is not quite lost. The evening before that last really bad frost is a very busy evening at our house. We harvest all the tomatoes that show even a hint of ripening — just that subtle change from dark green to yellow-green is enough. At least some of those tomatoes will ripen indoors. (If you like green tomato pickles or relish, grab a few of the really green tomatoes, too.) It's time to harvest all the winter squash and pumpkins; they'll go indoors overnight and then outdoors again on sunny, warm days to cure for storage.

▲ *The last harvest. Tomatoes can be picked green during the last days of warm weather and ripened on a windowsill.*

Do you have any broccoli or cabbage left? Time to harvest; the taste will be all the better because of the early, lighter frosts, but a really hard freeze will kill even somewhat hardy plants like these. Carrots will be safe in the soil for a while, but a layer of straw or a discarded blanket will ensure that they don't freeze.

Stowing Your Containers

Even if some, or many, of your containers come inside or continue in service with winter-hardy greens, many others are finished for the year and won't have anything growing in them until next spring. What to do with them? And what to do with the soil those containers contain?

Option 1: Let It Lie

This is the don't-do-much-of-anything option: Just tidy the containers a bit, cover them, and leave them where they are, full of soil. The plus side of this option is that it's not much work. This is how I deal with large or straight-sided containers. The soil in straight-sided containers is difficult to remove at the end of the season because you can't just tip over a container and dump it — the soil is a solid block of matter held together by plant roots and won't fall out easily. But by the time spring rolls around, much of the root mass will have been eaten by the soil dwellers that make compost, and the soil will be easier to remove or loosen for spring planting.

If you live in a region that doesn't experience harsh winters, this may be a good method for you. Your containers should be able to make it through the season without being damaged. In colder climates, however, the freezing and thawing that accompany winter months can wreak havoc on some kinds of containers (see box), especially those made of terra-cotta. When in doubt, bring it inside.

▲ *A winter rest. I leave my large self-watering containers outside for the winter, covered with a piece of plywood weighted with a brick.*

FROST-PROOF CONTAINERS

How frost-proof your container is will depend on what it's made from. Generally, terra-cotta and ceramic pots will not stand up to extreme freezing and thawing. In recent years, though, companies have begun to manufacture pots from fiberglass and foam that look like terra-cotta but can make it through the winter without cracking. Whiskey barrels and other wooden containers are better able to withstand the effects of winter, because they can expand and shrink with the seasons. Some kinds of sturdy plastic or resin can make it through unharmed.

If you're going to leave your containers out for the winter, leave the soil as dry as possible. Dry soil won't expand as it freezes and possibly damage a container. If you decide to try Option 1, follow these steps:

As soon as the plants are done producing, stop filling the reservoirs of self-watering containers. If you can do it without making a mess, remove any water left in the reservoir by tipping the container and letting the water run out.

Even if they have stopped producing, leave the plants in the container. They'll take water from the soil for transpiration and thereby reduce the moisture level of the soil. If rain threatens, cover the container.

When the plants have started to wilt or have been frosted, remove them. Pull up small ones, and clip big ones at soil level and leave the roots until spring; by then, soil creatures will have eaten all the hair roots.

Cover the planter for winter to keep out rain and snow. I use a piece of plywood weighted with a brick, but a tarp or plastic sheeting will also serve.

Option 2: Tip and Store

Although I like the simplicity of the "Let It Lie" method, I don't always do it this way. With most of my containers, I tip the container, empty the soil onto a tarp, and store it in a garbage can. I then wash the container thoroughly with soap and water and store it in the garden shed or the garage until spring. Simple as that.

This method has several benefits. My containers don't suffer from exposure to the elements. Also, containers of a similar shape nest together well and take up less space than they would if filled with soil. Preparing for spring is also simpler; the soil I've emptied out is much easier to mix amendments into when it's not caked to the container that housed it all winter.

◀ *Pulling up roots. Leaving plants in the container up until the very end helps dry out the soil for winter storage, but there comes a point when the green matter needs to go.*

Save That Soil!

Don't throw away the soil. It's not just as good as it was last spring, but it can be made to be just as good without much effort. After a summer of growing plants, the soil is not as fertile as it was; some of the capital in that account has been used up. There also isn't quite as much soil as there used to be; some of it has been eaten by soil dwellers and ultimately turned into nutrients to nourish the plants that grew there.

Replace What's Missing

To revitalize container soil and make it as good as new, just replace what has been used up. Most of the peat is still there: there are not many soil creatures who consider peat moss their favorite food. All the vermiculite and perlite are still there; *nobody* eats them. And some of the compost is gone, turned into plant food by soil-dwelling microbes.

How much compost is gone? How full was the container at the start of the season? How full is it at the end of the season? The difference is roughly the amount of compost that's been used up. The amount will vary depending on what grew in the container. I usually need to add about two to three quarts of compost to 40 quarts of container mix, then a cup of the same fertilizer mix I used when I first mixed the soil.

To get the garden going in the second and succeeding years, I mix in whatever ingredients I've chosen to renew the soil and then moisten the refreshed container soil the same way I did the first year.

In the spring, I take the soil out of the containers I've wintered over outside. It is much easier to remove the soil in the spring because it's dry and some of the roots holding it together have rotted away. Container soil that has dried thoroughly may contain hard lumps. Moisten the soil before you work it, and the lumps will be easy to break up.

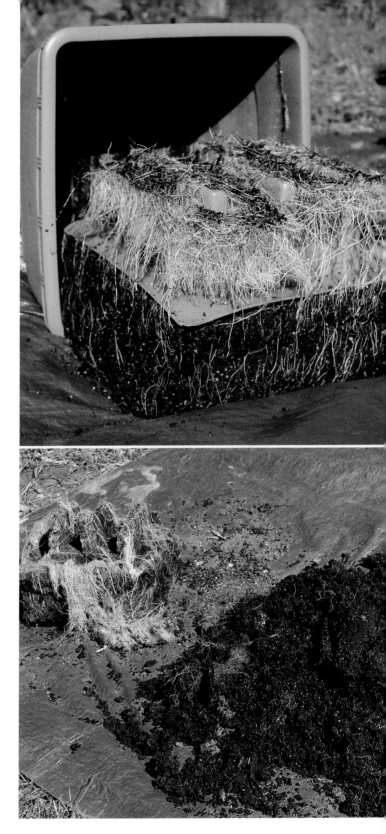

▲ *Tip it out. At the end of the season, empty and clean your containers for storage. Add the spent soil to the compost pile or put it aside to be combined with fresh compost and fertilizer mix for next spring's containers.*

PART THREE

Incredible Edibles

What to Grow?

Now, what to grow? And what size container to grow it in? Much of this will depend on the varieties of plants you choose. For instance, you can grow miniature 'Micro Tom' tomatoes in a window box or hanging planter, but you'll need a large self-watering container with lots of soil capacity to grow a full-size 'Brandywine'. Another consideration is how many containers you'll be gardening in this season. If you're starting with just one, you'll be better off with a container with lots of soil space, so that you have room to grow a few different kinds of plants if you choose to. The table at right gives specific dimensions for a few of the self-watering containers I've used (and which you see pictured throughout the book). As you read about the vegetables in this section, keep these container sizes in mind, especially the number and type of plants that can comfortably fit in each one. Happy gardening!

ED's PICK

BLUE-RIBBON EDIBLES

Conventional gardening wisdom tells us that although you *can* grow vegetables in containers, they won't grow nearly as well as they would if they were in the ground. After three years of trialing different edibles in self-watering containers, I realized that this conventional wisdom is not always true.

In fact, many vegetables I trialed actually grew *better* in self-watering containers than they did in my earth garden. Often these were vegetables that, in addition to thriving on the consistent moisture a self-watering container offers, grew better in the warmer soil of a container or enjoyed the lack of competition from weeds and other plants. Throughout this encyclopedia, I've indicated these plants with a blue ribbon. Sylvia and I now grow many of these edibles only in self-watering containers.

PICK YOUR POT

	DIMENSIONS inches (centimeters)		SOIL CAPACITY	RESERVOIR CAPACITY
	LENGTH x WIDTH	DEPTH	quarts (liters)	quarts (liters)
SMALL				
Hanging basket	12.5 diameter (31.7)	7 (17.8)	8 (8.8)	1 (1.1)
Window box (sm)	23 × 9 (58.4 × 28.6)	7.5 (19.1)	17 (18.7)	5.5 (6.1)
MEDIUM				
Provence planter	20 diameter (50.8)	14.75 (37.5)	30 (33)	4 (4.4)
Window box (lg)	39 × 9 (99.1 × 28.7)	7.5 (19.1)	28 (30.8)	9 (9.9)
LARGE				
Self-watering planter	26.25 × 19.25 (66.7 × 50.2)	10.5 (26.7)	40 (44)	16 (15.1)
DEEP				
Deep-root planter	19 × 19 (48.3 × 48.3)	14 (35.6)	30 (33)	13 (14.3)
Whiskey barrel	23.5 diameter (59.7)	16 (40.6)	45 (49.5)	32 (30.3)
Terrazza trough planter	39.25 × 16.5 (99.7 × 41.9)	18.5 (47)	130 (143)	16 (15.1)
MISC				
Strawberry planter	18 diameter (45.7)	18 (45.7)	30 (33)	4 (4.4)

CHAPTER TWELVE

THE BEST VEGETABLES

When I started growing vegetables in containers, I expected that I would have success with only some of the many edibles I have grown in my earth garden. To my surprise, I found that I could grow almost all of my earth garden favorites in containers. Some varieties of a vegetable grew better than others, but always there was a carrot or a tomato or a squash that yielded a satisfying harvest.

ARTICHOKES

(*Cynara scolymus*)

Artichokes were introduced to this country more than 80 years ago from Italy; with that balmy heritage, they're often difficult to grow in the ground in colder parts of the United States. But the same characteristics that make artichokes a challenge in many earth gardens make them happily at home in pots — soil warms more quickly in a container than it does in the ground. Artichokes are also very attractive plants and make a nice aesthetic addition to any container garden.

Artichokes are big plants and grow best alone in a medium or large self-watering container.

PICK YOUR POT

For artichokes, the rule of thumb is, "The bigger the container, the bigger the plant" — to a point. That point, in my experience, is around 30 quarts of soil capacity. Smaller than that yields a significantly smaller plant with smaller and fewer buds. Larger (40 quarts) yields a slightly but not significantly larger plant with about the same number and size of buds. The medium container is just enough lighter to make it portable, which is an advantage if you need to move it to get better sun exposure as the season progresses. Artichokes definitely do better in self-watering containers.

GROW IT

Artichokes are actually perennial plants in warm climates (USDA Zones 8 to 11), but most cold-climate gardeners grow them as annuals. If you're growing artichokes as annuals, you'll have to start your plants indoors in late winter in order to have a harvest. Sow the seeds about ¼ inch deep in flats or cells and keep the temperature between 70 and 80°F (21°C and 27°C) until germination, which usually takes about two weeks. Grow seedlings at 60–70°F (15–21°C) daytime and 50–60°F (10–15°C) nighttime temperatures, transplanting to a four-inch pot after the first true leaves appear. Transplant to an outdoor container when all danger of frost is past and soil temperature is above 60°F (15°C).

It's even easier to let someone else get the plants started. We're fortunate to have a nearby greenhouse where we can buy artichoke plants ready for transplanting and already growing in a compost-based, organic medium similar to the mix we use in our containers.

Thanks to their Mediterranean background, artichokes love sun. They're also big plants with a lot of biomass; they'll probably need extra fertilizer after six weeks of growth.

Eat It

The part we eat is actually the plant's flower bud, harvested quite a while before it is ready to burst forth as a large and spectacular bloom. Clip the flower buds with about an inch of stem. It is said that immature and very small buds are more tender and can be steamed and eaten whole. We wait a bit and let them reach a size of three to four inches in diameter but still with tight, firm scales. An artichoke is past its peak as soon as the scales begin to separate, the first sign that the flower bud has begun to open. The top bud is the first to mature and usually the largest.

Mature artichokes need to be steamed for 10 to 15 minutes before eating. Although many people only eat the heart of the artichoke, the insides of the scales also contain tender edible flesh. Try dipping the scales in mayonnaise and scraping out the flesh with your teeth. When you reach the interior of the artichoke, scoop out the thistly center and eat the heart and any tender parts of the stem.

Bug Off

In my experience, artichokes are not bothered by any pests or diseases in the home garden.

Pick Your Plant

'Green Globe': deep green buds; a good choice for gardeners in warm climates

'Imperial Star': designed to be grown as an annual and will produce reliably in all but the shortest of growing seasons; does not need to "chill out" (see "A Time to Chill," this page) in order to produce flower buds.

'Violetto': violet, rather than green, buds; hardy to Zone 6

The top bud of this 'Imperial Star' artichoke is ready for harvest.

A TIME TO CHILL

In its natural habitat, an artichoke, after growing through its first summer, experiences a winter of cool (below 50°F [10°C]) but not freezing temperatures. That cool winter convinces the plant that it's two years old and ready to produce flowers. To trigger the budding response during the first year of an artichoke's life (for varieties other than 'Imperial Star'), grow the plants within a temperature range of 35°F to 50°F (2 to 10°C) for at least 10 days. If you can't prevent the temperature from exceeding 50, run the cold treatment for a longer time.

ARUGULA

(*Eruca vesicaria* subsp. *sativa*)

For those who really like arugula — also called roquette or rocket — there is no substitute. The leaves are tender to the tooth but variously described as pungent, peppery, nutty, or tangy and add a unique taste to salad. The leaves develop a more pungent taste after the plant bolts, but some people like this. The white flowers are edible as well.

Harvest arugula leaves when they are four to six inches long, or wait and harvest the whole plant.

CULINARY COUSINS

Gardeners with a bolder taste should try Italian arugula (*Diplotaxis tenuifolia*). A smaller plant that's slower growing, Italian arugula has more deeply lobed leaves, and yellow flowers. It is less likely than the garden-variety arugula to bolt in warm weather. Its taste is initially more pungent but changes less when the plant bolts. The flowers are also edible.

PICK YOUR POT

Grow in the same containers you would use for other salad greens — a window box or a large self-watering container.

GROW IT

Arugula is easy to grow and makes a good container plant. Space seeds closely for baby greens or about six inches apart for harvest as mature plants. Succession plantings two or three weeks apart will keep you in greens until (or, in the case of Italian arugula, right through) summer. Sow about ¼ inch deep in early spring. Arugula, like other salad greens, prefers cool weather and will bolt in summer, especially if it is planted thickly, as it is for cut-and-come-again harvesting. To postpone bolting, shade the plants during hot weather.

EAT IT

Harvest leaves when they are about four to six inches long, or harvest the whole plant later by pulling it or cutting just below soil level. Arugula is fairly hardy and, when sown in late summer or early fall, can be harvested into early winter.

BUG OFF

Arugula is highly prized by flea beetles. If your containers are on a porch or a patio, flea beetles might not find them, but if you are visited by these voracious little pests, grow arugula under a row cover. Raising containers off the ground and keeping them away from thickets of brush and weeds may deter flea beetle invasions.

BEANS

(*Phaseolus* spp. and *Vicia faba*)

There's more to beans than most of us realize. Before there are beans on the plant, there are very pretty edible flowers in shades of white, red, and purple. There are snap beans (the ones we usually see at the market), but there are also filet beans, shell beans, and pole beans. Whichever kind you decide to grow, you'll soon realize that garden-fresh beans taste much better than those that are even a few hours old.

PICK YOUR POT

Beans and self-watering containers were made for each other. A large rectangular container can be home to a dozen and a half bush bean plants, each loaded with beans you can harvest at just the right maturity and eat when they are really fresh. To stay healthy and yield well, bean plants need water all the time.

GROW IT

For a little word, *beans* covers a whole lot of ground. The major division for beans refers to their growth habit, as either bushes (bush beans) or vines (pole beans). Either type can be grown in containers, but pole beans will need a trellis to grow on.

Pole beans produce over a longer time and, because they're bigger plants, produce more beans per plant than bush beans. But pole beans are *big* plants. In the earth garden they'll climb as far as a trellis will allow, and then they keep growing anyway, forming a massive and heavy clump at the top. A trellis for pole beans needs to be strong and very well anchored. I grow 'Scarlet Runner' beans on a trellis that forms an arch connecting two containers. The arch, covered with dark green leaves and (edible) red flowers, serves as an entrance to the container garden.

Beans are not happy in cold weather. (The exception is fava beans, which don't just tolerate cold soil, they *prefer* it. Plant them when you'd plant peas.) Most beans are not just frost sensitive, they're also cold sensitive, and they don't care to grow in soil that is colder than 60°F (15°C). Optimum germination temperature is 70–90°F (21–32°C). Beans planted in cool soil germinate more slowly and are, later in life, more susceptible to disease. Having gotten off to a poor start, they never really catch up, and won't grow as quickly or produce as well.

You can, as a container gardener, cheat the calendar a bit by starting your beans in a container indoors and moving everything outdoors when temperatures get up to 60°F (15°C).

Like all pole beans, these 'Scarlet Runner' vines need a sturdy trellis well anchored to the container or to the earth.

(This works only if you can move the container around. Plan to use a smaller and lighter container for early beans or on enlisting some strong helpers to move larger containers.)

Sow bean seeds about four inches apart and an inch deep after the danger of frost is past and temperatures are dependably above 65°F (18°C). That's it. Beans are easy keepers. Just keep the reservoir full, and when it's time to harvest, pick often.

EAT IT

Beans are at their peak of flavor for only a short time. *Snap beans* vary in mature length depending on the variety, but they're all at their prime of flavor when they're about ¼ inch or just a bit more in diameter. At that stage the seeds have not started to swell and the pod is uniformly smooth. Bean pods grow quickly; expect to harvest at least every third day. Regular harvests both yield the best-tasting beans and stimulate the plants to further production. (Snap beans left too long on the plant can be left still longer and harvested as shell beans when the beans within the pod are plump.) *Filet beans* look like snap beans, but they're not. If you let a filet bean grow to the proper size for a snap bean, it will be tough, stringy, and not worth eating. Filet beans are at their peak of flavor when they're only about ⅛ inch in diameter. Harvest filet beans daily or every other day. *Shell beans* are ripe for eating when the beans are plump in the pods. For my money, shell beans are just as tasty as lima beans, and they're a lot easier to grow, especially in cooler parts of the country.

BUG OFF

Beans are easy to grow and usually free from disease. Possibilities for disease increase sharply if the plants are handled while the leaves are wet from dew or rain. Postpone harvesting until the leaves are dry. Mexican bean beetles may be a problem if you live in the East or the Southwest. These pests can be excluded with row covers, repelled by reflective mulch (aluminum foil), or killed by a botanical pesticide. (See chapter nine.)

PICK YOUR PLANT

FILET BEANS (HARICOTS VERTS)

These look superficially like regular green beans, but they're meant to be harvested much smaller than other beans. Picked when they should be picked, filet beans are in a taste class all their own and sell in upscale markets and restaurants at a price commensurate with their flavor.

'**Maxibel**': slender, seven-inch beans that don't develop strings, meaning you can get away with a little longer span between pickings

'**Straight 'n' Narrow**': tasty bean on a compact plant, and, just as the name suggests, very straight; consistent blue-ribbon winners for us at the county fair

THE BENEFITS OF INOCULANTS

Beans and peas can form a special relationship with certain soil-dwelling bacteria: the bean or pea plant allows the bacteria to live within its roots, where they form nodules that capture nitrogen from the air. This symbiotic relationship can supply most of the nitrogen the plant needs for growth. Although these bacteria — called rhizobia — are naturally occurring in the soil, there generally aren't enough of them. Gardeners can correct the deficiency by inoculating seeds with bacteria. The inoculant comes as a powder to be applied to the seeds or as granules to be sprinkled in the furrow before planting the seeds.

SNAP BEANS

These are your standard, garden-variety beans, usually in shades of green, but also yellow or purple. (The purple ones turn green when cooked.)

'**Jade**': compact plants and exceptional flavor

'**Provider**': easy to grow, even when the weather is not ideally sunny and warm; germinates better in cool soil than other beans do

'**Rocdor**': a yellow, or wax, bean with straight pods; germinates in cool soil

'**Royal Burgundy**': dark purple when raw but green when cooked

SHELL BEANS

Like peas, shell beans are grown for the seeds inside the pod, not for the pod and seeds together.

'**Flagrano**': French flageolet bean that's easy to shell; can also be used as a dry bean

'**Tongue of Fire**': attractive red-streaked pods with good flavor and texture; can be used as a snap bean if harvested young

POLE BEANS

If you choose to grow these in a container, be sure to give them a sturdy trellis to climb. There are many pole bean varieties, but I find most of them too large to grow in containers.

'**Scarlet Runner**': a beautiful plant with gorgeous flowers. It's edible in many stages: as flowers, snap beans, shell beans, and, if you have some left at the end of the season, dry beans

The flowers and pods of purple-podded pole bean are edible.

Eighteen of these very prolific 'Straight 'n' Narrow' bean plants will fit in a large self-watering container.

BEETS

(*Beta vulgaris*)

Beets are a multipurpose vegetable at many stages of growth. Seedlings just two or three inches tall are a fine addition to spring salads. Later, when the greens are six to eight inches tall but the beet itself hasn't started to develop, you can steam up a mess of greens. The beets are edible alone (and the tops have become a bit tough) when they are about an inch and a half in diameter, and that's when I think they taste best.

Because one beet seed is really a group of two to six seeds, beets naturally grow very close together.

PICK YOUR POT

Beets grow best and taste best when they grow fast, so they need rich soil and plenty of water; they turn woody and bitter if they lack water at any time. With needs like that, beets are a natural for self-watering containers. Because they have a long taproot, they do best in deeper containers, 10–12 inches deep.

GROW IT

Although I have read that beets can be started indoors and transplanted, I've never seen the need to do so and therefore haven't tried it. I seed beets half an inch deep and two (for greens) or three (for beets) inches apart directly in the container they'll live in. The first planting can be a month before the last frost, with small succession plantings every two weeks. Although they like to grow in cool weather, beets germinate best in fairly warm soil. Preheat the container soil by covering it with black plastic or IRT (red plastic mulch).

Each beet "seed" is actually a cluster of seeds, so no matter how carefully the seeds are spaced, beets will emerge as a clump of plants. You can thin some of the plants to give more space to the survivors, but beets are used to growing in clustered conditions, and they'll do fine even if you don't thin them, especially if you harvest some of the crop early for greens. If you decide to thin, do it with scissors, clipping the unwanted plants at soil level; the roots of the plants in any cluster are thoroughly intertwined, and any attempt to thin by pulling the extra plants will disturb the roots of the plants you want to save.

EAT IT

For greens or baby-beets-and-greens, just pull the plants in clumps. For mature beets, after the greens are no longer tasty, pull the beets and trim the tops to about an inch long. (If the tops are trimmed close to the beet, the beet will "bleed.")

Bug Off

Provided they have enough water — the lack of which can cause scab — beets are easy keepers and unlikely to be bothered by pests or diseases.

Pick Your Plant

"He became red as a beet." How often have we read or heard that simile? As it turns out, not all beets are red, and if they are, they're not always red all the way through. Some beets are golden, some white, and some deep purple. Some, when sliced open, are striped, alternating rings of pink and white or light and dark red.

'**Big Top**': often grown primarily for its greens; harvest when the tops are full and the beets still tiny

'**Blankoma**': white; makes an interesting pickle

'**Bull's Blood**': red, but striped in cross-section, with dark red and light red alternating; leaves are red and good either cooked or in salads

'**Chioggia**': light red on the outside and striped on the inside, alternating rings of pink and white

'**Early Wonder Tall Top**': an heirloom variety especially good when harvested for greens with young beets (pictured below)

'**Golden Beet**': gold inside with orange skin, and in all other ways, a beet

Golden beets have the color of carrots but the look and taste of beets.

These 'Chioggia' beets look like any ordinary variety until you cut them open. Surprise!

BROCCOLI

(*Brassica oleracea*, Italica Group)

Healthful (lots of vitamin A and calcium), tasty, easy to grow, and very much at home in containers, broccoli is a fine addition to any container vegetable garden. Any full-size broccoli will grow well in a large enough container, but I usually grow the mini varieties that are happy in smaller spaces.

Although full-size broccoli will grow in a medium-size container, I prefer the more compact 'Munchkin'.

CULINARY COUSIN

Broccoli raab, a close relative of broccoli, does not form heads and has a more pungent taste. The young stems, leaves, and flower buds are the edible parts, and are often eaten raw in salads, steamed, or stir-fried. Because it is prey to flea beetles and does not like heat, broccoli raab is best grown in late summer for a fall harvest.

PICK YOUR POT

We grow two compact plants in a medium-size self-watering container.

GROW IT

For an early crop, start broccoli indoors and transplant to containers two to four weeks before the last frost. Broccoli is tolerant of some frost at either end of its growing year, but protecting the plants with row covers on chilly nights is a good idea.

EAT IT

Broccoli heads — really clusters of flower buds — are best harvested when the buds are still dark green and show no sign of opening. (A yellowish color signals that the head is past its culinary prime.) Most varieties will then produce many smaller side shoots. Harvest these regularly and still more will grow. Cut the main head on a slant, so that water flows off the cut stem; the stem will be less likely to rot.

BUG OFF

Flea beetles can decimate young broccoli plants. Cabbage caterpillars don't do much damage, but they're not fun to find in your meal. Bt carefully applied will kill the caterpillars without harming other insects. Row covers are a good way to protect against flea beetles after planting and against caterpillars later on.

PICK YOUR PLANT

'**Arcadia**': my favorite full-size broccoli; prefers a medium or large container

'**Munchkin**': grows a 4-inch head on a 12-inch plant and then produces loads of side shoots right into the cool days of autumn

'**Small Miracle**': yields a slightly larger head than 'Munchkin' on a similar-size plant

BRUSSELS SPROUTS

(*Brassica oleracea*, Gemmifera Group)

For a good fall crop, not much beats Brussels sprouts. The plants survive frosts and continue to grow and ripen their sprouts far into the fall of the year. The sprouts actually taste better after they have been frosted a couple of times. Brussels sprouts do take a long time to grow and produce a crop, but if you've got the space, they're worth a try.

PICK YOUR POT

There's a lot of plant material in a Brussels sprout plant; it needs room to grow a substantial root system and needs plenty of food and water. A single plant can grow in a medium self-watering container; two or three can share a large container.

GROW IT

Brussels sprouts can be direct-seeded in warm climates (at least a four-month frost-free growing season), but should be started indoors in northern regions. Start seeds indoors four to six weeks before the last frost date. Transplant when the seedlings are four to six weeks old. In warmer climes, direct-seed Brussels sprouts about two weeks before the last frost date, when the soil temperature is at least 50°F (10°C). Germination takes about a week at 75°F (24°C), longer at lower temperatures.

Growing Brussels sprouts under a row cover has two major benefits: it raises the temperature somewhat and thereby promotes faster early growth and it protects the plants from flea beetles. Brussels sprouts are heavy feeders, especially of phosphorus. Add about ⅓ cup of soft rock phosphate (also known as colloidal phosphate) or steamed bonemeal to each 40 quarts of container mix. If your plants grow too slowly or the leaves develop a purple color, fertilize with liquid fish emulsion every two weeks.

To get an earlier and more even harvest, about a month before the first hard freeze (less than 25°F [3.8°C]), remove the growing tip of the plant (a rosette of small leaves at the very top). This encourages the plant to concentrate all its energy on maturing the sprouts it's already set, instead of making more.

Two or three 'Oliver' Brussels sprout plants can grow together in a large container.

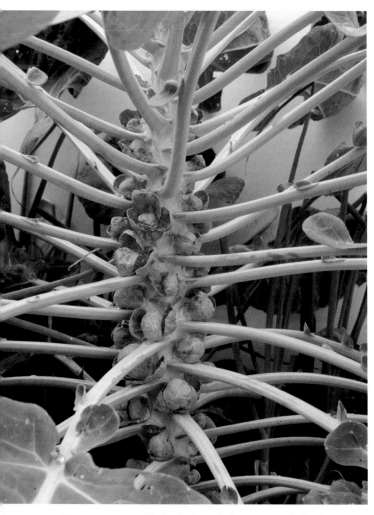

The sprouts on this 'Jade Cross' plant are ready for harvest when they are the size of a marble.

EAT IT

The sprouts are ready to harvest when they are half an inch to an inch in diameter and still firm. They are past their prime when they begin to open and lose their firmness. Start the harvest at the base of the stem and work upward as the sprouts mature.

Break off the leaf just below the sprout, then twist off or cut the sprout. If some sprouts remain on the plant when a hard frost is due, cut the whole plant, remove the leaves, and store it in a cool, damp place like a root cellar. Alternatively, you can harvest all the sprouts and freeze them.

BUG OFF

Like all their brassica cousins, Brussels sprouts are a favorite food of flea beetles, especially when they're young and tender. The best way to solve the problem is to prevent it. Grow plants under row covers for at least the first month they are outdoors. (Put on the covers as soon as you transplant; otherwise flea beetles will be on them within hours.) Although Brussels sprouts are said to be prey to other cabbage-family pests, I have not had any problems other than flea beetles with container-grown plants.

PICK YOUR PLANT

The so-called dwarf varieties, while still substantial plants, are the best choices for container growing.

'Jade cross': short-season F1 hybrid

'Oliver': short-season F1 hybrid; easy to grow, matures early

HIGH WIND ALERT

Brussels sprout plants can grow as tall as three feet and have a lot of foliage at the top, making them susceptible to wind damage. If your plants must grow where they will encounter high or steady winds, consider growing them inside a square or rectangular cage, like the ones used for tomatoes.

CABBAGE

(*Brassica oleracea*, Capitata Group)

Because of its large size, cabbage is not usually recommended for container growing. Fortunately, some dwarf varieties are the size of a softball and meant for eating fresh. These mini cabbages are very nice container plants and are welcome additions to late-summer salads at a time when other salad greens are well past their prime.

PICK YOUR POT

You can grow up to six dwarf varieties in a large self-watering container. Space them closely to keep heads small.

GROW IT

For a summer crop, start seeds four to six weeks before the last expected spring frost. Sow the seeds about half an inch deep, two or three seeds per cell. Cabbage seeds germinate best at around 75°F (24°C). When the seedlings emerge, thin to a single seedling, lower the temperature to 60°F (15°C), and keep it there until it's time to transplant. Space plants about eight inches apart.

EAT IT

Cut the heads at soil level as soon as they reach a harvestable size. (This will vary depending on the variety.)

BUG OFF

Flea beetles can set back seedlings, but they lose interest when the plants age and become tougher to munch on. Protect with row covers right from the moment of planting.

Green cabbages, but not reds, are also prey to the dreaded cabbage caterpillar. Cover the plants with a row cover when those pretty white butterflies are flitting around, so they can't lay the eggs that will become the voracious caterpillars.

PICK YOUR PLANT

'Alcosa': a savoy; when spaced about eight inches apart, produces single-serving heads.

'Arrowhead': green, but cone shaped rather than round

'Gonzales': round and green with a sweetly spicy taste

'Red Express': round and red; compact plant with small head

'Gonzales' produces a small, four- to six-inch head on a compact plant that's perfect for containers.

Red cabbages, unlike their green cousins, are not bothered by cabbage caterpillars.

CARROTS

(*Daucus carota* var. *sativa*)

I *f the carrot of your dreams is upwards of 10 inches long, you may wonder if you can grow carrots in a container. Fortunately, some are quite content to be around six inches and others, the baby or mini varieties, are small enough to grow in just about any container. If you choose the right variety, carrots are actually easier to grow in containers than they are in your earth garden, because they thrive on steady moisture, especially during their long and potentially difficult germination period.*

Thin your carrots so that they have the space they need to grow to whatever you want to call "harvest size."

PICK YOUR POT

Carrots don't compete well with other plants, so they do best when they grow only among other carrots. Shorter and mini varieties can grow in most self-watering containers with a soil depth of at least 8 inches, but I recommend deep (10–12 inches of soil) containers for any standard-size carrots.

GROW IT

Carrots are among the easiest and most trouble-free vegetables once they get a start in life — but getting that start is not easy. Carrot seeds are tiny, so they have to be sown close to the surface, no more than ¼ to ½ inch deep, and they need to be moist all the time in order to germinate. In an earth garden, it is difficult to keep the soil moist during all of the fairly long (one to three weeks) germination period. But in a self-watering container, it's easy. As a result, carrots germinate faster and get a better start in life.

Sow carrot seeds about ½ inch apart. No, let's get real: *try to* sow carrot seeds about ½ inch apart. There are all sorts of inventive seeding devices and many paragraphs in garden books devoted to solving the mystery of *how* one can get those tiny, impossible-to-grasp seeds accurately spaced. Don't worry. It's not going happen. No matter how hard you try, some of those carrot seeds will end up in little clusters. You'll have to thin the resulting plants so that only one remains every ½ inch or so. I do the initial thinning with scissors, cutting off the extra plants at the soil line. That way I don't disturb the roots of the plants I want to save. The little bit of carrot that stays behind in the soil is soon consumed by bacteria and becomes plant food for the survivors. Later on I'll do a second thinning to leave about an inch between plants. This time I pull the unwanted plants:

they're far enough from their neighbors that no damage is done. I postpone this thinning until the baby carrots are deep orange and therefore tasty; they go into a salad as the first harvest from the carrot patch.

Eat It

Carrots are good to eat as soon as their characteristic deep orange color develops. (Actually, not all carrots are orange; some are red, some purple, and some yellow. Let's say that carrots are good to eat when they have fully developed their *color*, whatever that color is.) They're edible before that, but they're not very tasty. I grow a lot of carrots in the earth garden for winter storage, but in the container garden I'm growing carrots for fresh eating, mostly raw in salads. I like raw carrots best while they are still young and tender, so I generally harvest the container carrots before they reach full size. A series of small succession plantings three weeks apart will keep you in tasty, fresh carrots all summer.

Bug Off

Grown in fertile soil, carrots are rarely prey to insect pests or disease. If carrot rust fly and wireworms invade your carrot patch, keep out the adults that lay the eggs by using row covers.

Pick Your Plant

'Kinko': easy to grow, sweet, and early; best when harvested young; only four inches long, so they're perfect for fairly shallow containers

'Mokum': a tasty, sweet carrot for fresh eating

'Nelson': sweet, not too long, and early

'Parmex': cute, little round carrots that can grow in most any container; harvest when they are about 1½ inches in diameter

'Purple Haze': six- to seven-inch carrot with purple skin and an orange interior

'Yellowstone': butter yellow and about eight inches long

'Kinko' (left) and 'Parmex' are mini carrots, perfect for container growing.

'Purple Haze' can reach six or more inches (plus a tap root), and needs a container that's about a foot deep.

CAULIFLOWER

(*Brassica oleracea*, Botrytis Group)

The cauliflower we see in stores is white — a bit bland, perhaps, for a colorful container garden. But white's not all there is to cauliflower, not by a long shot. How about green? Or orange? Or purple! The orange stays orange when cooked, getting even brighter; the green stays green; the purple turns bluish. In addition to color, the nonwhite cauliflowers have another advantage: they needn't be blanched (see "Blanching," next page).

Its curd still tight, this 'Snow Crown' cauliflower is ready to be harvested now.

'Violet Queen' has the taste of cauliflower and the look of broccoli but a color all its own.

PICK YOUR POT

Cauliflower grows best among its own kind, free from competition. Single plants can thrive in medium self-watering containers, or plant four in a large container.

GROW IT

Although it is not difficult to grow, cauliflower has a well-deserved reputation for being a bit fussy. Like many biennials we gardeners grow as annuals, cauliflower gets confused when stressed, thinks that it's in its second year, and bolts. Fortunately, there are several things you can do to avoid stressing a cauliflower.

First, transplant it carefully so as not to disturb the roots. Plan to transplant seedlings outdoors when they are four or five weeks old; plants older than that are more likely to be stressed by transplanting. They're also apt to become root-bound, a condition called "checking," after which they produce only tiny heads. Also be sure to transplant seedlings after the danger of frost is past, and protect them with row covers on cool nights.

If you're starting plants indoors, sow seed ¼ to ½ inch deep in four-inch pots. Keep soil temperature between 70 and 80°F (21–27°C) until they emerge, then 60 to 70°F (15–21°C).

Once seedlings are established in their new home, make sure there is always water in the container reservoir. Move the container to a cool spot if summer weather is very hot for very long. Also protect plants from fall frost; among cabbage-family cousins, cauliflower is the most sensitive to frost.

Eat It

Cut the heads as soon as they are large enough, before there is any separation of the curd. (You'll probably wait too long until you fine-tune your sense of when to harvest. A little too soon is better than a little too late.) Once the head starts to develop, check daily.

Bug Off

Like its cabbage-family cousins, cauliflower attracts flea beetles, especially when the plants are young. The best remedy is prevention: grow cauliflower under row covers at least until the plants are old and tough enough that flea beetles have gone on to other restaurants. If you don't use row covers, refer to chapter nine for ways to kill the little hoppers.

Cauliflower is also prey to cabbage worms, though seldom to the same degree as cabbage and broccoli are. Row covers are the best solution here too, though the caterpillar damage is usually minimal and can safely be ignored.

Pick Your Plant

'**Cheddar**': orange!

'**Graffiti**': purple!

'**Panther**': lime green florets (below); a big plant, so don't skimp on space for it — heads can grow to a foot in diameter

'**Snow Crown**': easy to grow and more tolerant of stress than most other cauliflower types

'**Violet Queen**': broccoli-like heads that are purple, turning to green when cooked. Excellent when used raw in salads.

BLANCHING

White cauliflower looks — and, most would say, tastes — better if the head is protected from the sun as it develops. As soon as the head starts to show through the leaves, gather outer leaves to cover the head and secure with string or a rubber band. The head will stay white rather than turn yellow from exposure to the sun.

After the blanching has begun, take a daily peek beneath the leaves to assess the head development. The key to tasty cauliflower is timely harvest, while the curd is still firm and tight.

CELERY

(*Apium graveolens* var. *dulce*)

*C*elery is a small but steady part of our diet, finding its way into salads, sandwiches, soups, and
casseroles. I think the celery we grow tastes better than what we can buy, and that's reason
enough to grow a few plants in our container garden. Because it's sensitive to drought, celery has
a reputation for being a bit difficult to grow, especially in dry climates or short growing seasons.
But the very qualities that make it fussy in earth gardens make it a very good candidate for self-
watering containers.

*This is actually two celery plants, a green and a red. Both
are somewhat smaller than they would be if grown alone
in a container of this size.*

PICK YOUR POT

Celery has a compact root system, much of which is near the
soil surface. If water is not nearby and continually present, it
suffers. If the soil surface dries out, the celery roots in that soil
die. If other plants grow too near and compete for water and
food, celery suffers. This is a plant designed for life in a self-
watering container filled with a rich, compost-based soil. The
soil is always moist all the way to the soil surface, and there's
always plenty of food.

I usually grow a single celery plant all by itself in a medium
self-watering container, but I've also had success growing it with
a pepper plant and an eggplant or a very compact tomato in a
large, rectangular planter. It also grows nicely surrounded by
small beet greens, as seen on page 91.

GROW IT

Celery seeds are tiny. Therefore, they have to be very close to
the soil surface (⅛ inch deep) to germinate. Celery seeds must
stay moist in order to germinate; that means that the soil they
are planted in must be moist all the way to the surface and stay
that way for the two or three weeks germination requires. Celery also needs warmth; it germinates best at about 75˚F (24˚C).
Sow the seeds half an inch apart 10–12 weeks before the last
frost date in a small flat (cottage cheese containers work well,
as do plastic seeding flats about five inches square). Place the
flat in a plastic bag to keep the soil from drying out, then put
the whole package in a warm place. Keep the soil moist and
70–75˚F (21–24˚C) through the long germination period. After
the seeds sprout, reduce temperatures to 60–70˚F (15–21˚C).
Celery exposed to temperatures below 55˚F (13˚C) for 10 days
or more may bolt later in the year. Celery can survive light frosts
in the fall if protected by a row cover.

When the plants have two true leaves, transplant them to two-inch pots or cells. I move them to a self-watering starting tray because it's easier to keep the soil moist. Grow at temperatures above 60°F. Transplant outdoors when the danger of frost is past and the weather is dependably warm, with daytime temperatures consistently above 55°F (13°C) and night temperatures of at least 40°F (4°C). Celery is an easy keeper once it gets going, but it is a heavy feeder and may benefit from periodic snacks of liquid seaweed fertilizer.

EAT IT

You can harvest stalks from the outside of the plant whenever they are big enough to suit you, or wait longer and cut the whole plant at soil level. Celery can tolerate a light frost if protected by a row cover, but plan to harvest it or move plants inside before a hard frost. We grow a few plants in portable, medium-size containers and move them indoors for the winter. (As I'm writing, in early April, there's one in a sunny kitchen window. When spring fully arrives, the plants go right on living, but — true to their biennial nature — soon bolt.)

BUG OFF

Although some gardeners report problems with aphids, I've never had anything bother a celery plant. Check plants for aphids and if they are present in large numbers, refer to chapter nine for remedies.

PICK YOUR PLANT

'Conquistador': a Utah type noted for its taste; able to tolerate a bit more adversity than can some other celeries

'Redventure': a cross between 'Ventura' and the heirloom 'Giant Red'; provides a spot of color with tender red stalks and emerald green leaves

'Ventura': dependable and easy to grow once it gets past the fussy germination stage; disease resistant with an upright growth habit and a tender heart; dark green leaves and stalks

CULINARY COUSINS

It sounds a bit like *celery* and looks a bit like it, too, but celeriac is more than a homely little brother to celery. The secret to celeriac's success is the bulblike formation just below its cluster of stalks. The bulb is edible; it can be grated or diced and added to soups or salad or baked whole. But the bulb can also be saved in a cool place and forced in the doldrums of winter. Plant the bulblike root in a pot of damp sand, and keep the sand moist. Soon you'll be rewarded with small, flavorful, celery-like stalks and leaves.

Celery is bred to produce stalks; celeriac is bred for its tasty bulblike root.

CHINESE CABBAGE

ED'S PICK

(*Brassica rapa*)

Although it's called cabbage and is a member of the brassica clan, this Asian branch of the family has more in common with romaine lettuce than it does with other cabbages. It looks a lot like a romaine, but with crinklier leaves. And although it can be cooked, it is also quite tasty raw in a salad. That's the way we like it.

Chinese cabbage fills our salad bowl in the heat of summer, when lettuces have long since ceased to prosper. Flea beetles often plague young plants, but can be excluded by using a protective row cover.

PICK YOUR POT

Chinese cabbage has a relatively compact root system that grows close to the soil surface, making it a very good candidate for self-watering containers, where it gets the steady water it needs. Grow four to six plants per large container.

GROW IT

Chinese cabbage is happy to germinate in the warmer temperatures of late spring and early summer, and actually does best after the summer solstice. The result? A steady supply of salad greens at times when lettuces are generally not dependable.

Sow seeds about a month before the last frost date in two-inch pots or cells, planting two seeds per cell half an inch deep. Thin to one plant per cell after they emerge. Transplant when night temperatures are above 50°F (10°C) and the plants have 8–10 leaves. Or you can direct-seed after the frost danger is past, two or three seeds a foot apart; thin to one plant after emergence.

BUG OFF

Flea beetles love all brassicas, especially when they are young and tender. Cover plants with lightweight row covers as soon as transplants go into the container or the first seedlings emerge. It's also possible to avoid the problem by planting later in the season, when flea beetles are scarcer. We plant in midsummer for a fall crop, and by the time the seedlings are up, the flea beetles are gone for the year (unless it's been a very damp season).

EAT IT

Cut the whole plant as soon as it is large enough to suit you. Discard the outer leaves.

PICK YOUR PLANT

'**Minuet**': small heads (nine inches high) and bolt resistant

'**Rubicon**': 12-inch heads, bolt resistant

CLAYTONIA

(*Claytonia perfoliata*)

Miner's lettuce, it is sometimes called. And, no, I don't know why. Claytonia doesn't look or taste a bit like lettuce, but it is a very versatile and tasty addition to salads. It is truly a green for all seasons, and can survive temperatures of –20°F (–29°C) or lower in an unheated greenhouse.

PICK YOUR POT

Claytonia will grow in any container and is content to share a pot with other plants. Or you can fill a medium self-watering container or a window box with it and plan on continuing the harvest into late fall and early winter.

GROW IT

Claytonia is easy to grow — so easy, in fact, that it will self-seed and take over a container if you let it. It's easier to grow claytonia than it is to stop claytonia from growing.

Direct-seed about ¼ inch deep and an inch or so apart in rows six inches apart. Thin to six inches apart. (Toss the thinnings into a salad; the roots are edible too.) Alternatively, you can start two or three seeds per cell in a starting tray and transplant carefully, about six inches apart, to a container. Claytonia is happy growing by itself or with other salad greens like lettuce and spinach, but it will take over if you don't prune it back.

As the plant matures, a small white flower grows from the center of each pair of leaves. Bolting does not affect claytonia's flavor; add the flowers to your salad along with the leaves.

BUG OFF

If there's a pest or disease that favors claytonia, I've yet to encounter it.

EAT IT

Clip the leaves, including the stems, as soon as the leaves are large enough to bother with; the plant will go right on producing more and more.

Although it will survive throughout the growing season, claytonia does not taste as good in the heat of summer. Move its container to a cool place when the weather heats up. In winter, claytonia is happy indoors, preferably in a spot with sunlight but not a lot of heat.

Claytonia's bright green leaves and tiny white flowers brighten a salad in almost any month.

CORN

(*Zea mays*)

*C*orn is among the crops that container-gardening gurus will tell you not to bother with. Some corn varieties are smaller than others, though, and worth a try in containers. They taste great, they're fun to grow, and you'll have neighbors slack-jawed in disbelief when you tell them you're growing corn in a container on your porch.

The ears on this 'Delectable' corn have just begun to show silk, and can be harvested as baby corn. You could also leave them to mature, for some really fresh corn on the cob.

PICK YOUR POT

Corn needs a large self-watering container.

HOW TO

Plant corn only after soil temperatures are dependably above 65°F (18°C). Space the seeds about two inches apart and thin to four inches. You can get a dozen plants into a large container.

BUG OFF

Even container-grown corn can become supper for a raccoon. I keep coons from the corn with an electric fence. Alternatively, you could move the container to a safe place overnight, starting a few days before the corn is ready for harvest.

EAT IT

For mature corn, harvest when the kernels are full and ooze "milk" when punctured. At this stage, two to three weeks after the silks first appear, the silks are usually dry and brown rather than light green. Corn harvested in the morning, before the sun hits it, is sweeter than corn harvested later in the day.

Harvest baby corn just as the silks emerge. At that point, they're about the size of a finger and can be eaten raw. Harvesting at that stage also stimulates production of new ears.

PICK YOUR PLANT

'Delectable': bicolor sweet corn that can be harvested as baby corn or left to mature

'Golden Bantam': an old-time yellow corn with seven-inch ears on stalks five or six feet tall

'Luther Hill': an old-time, open-pollinated, white sweet corn producing three- to six-inch ears on stalks only four feet tall

CRESS

(*Lepidium sativum*)

Cress won't win any beauty contests, but its tangy, spicy crunch is a welcome addition to any dish. It's also incredibly easy to grow; if you're planting your first container garden, you ought to include some cress in your plans.

PICK YOUR POT

Choose a self-watering container that will accommodate the amount of cress you want to grow.

GROW IT

Cress is so easy to grow, it almost grows itself. Just sprinkle the seeds in a container, cover with a thin layer of container mix, wait a couple of weeks, and start the harvest. Any container will do. Some people even grow cress in a flat. Just keep it watered. A series of small succession plantings 10 days apart will keep your salad bowl full.

BUG OFF

The tangy taste of cress seems to deter any pests.

EAT IT

Cress is harvestable from when the first true leaves appear to when it reaches maturity (in about three weeks). Curly cress may bolt in warm weather, so plantings in spring or fall provide the best eating.

PICK YOUR PLANT

Curly cress: curly, bright green leaves with ruffled edges

Upland cress: rosettes of dark green, rounded leaves

Easy to grow and easy to tend, cress is a welcome addition to any summer salad.

CULINARY COUSIN

Watercress (*Nasturtium officinale*), as the name suggests, is a big-time water lover. Grow it in a self-watering container with a big enough reservoir so that the soil never dries no matter what fluctuations occur in your watering schedule. This otherwise easy-to-grow perennial has one additional requirement: soil a bit sweeter (pH near 7.0) than most garden vegetables need. Compost buffers the effects of less-than-perfect pH; I have not had problems growing watercress or any other edible in the compost-based container mixes I use.

CUCUMBER

(*Cucumis sativus*)

*C*ucumbers aren't difficult to grow, but they're a bit more demanding than some other vegetables. They like heat. They need a consistent supply of food (and thrive in a compost-based potting soil). Cucumbers also need water, and lots of it. That's sometimes difficult to provide in the garden, but it's easy in a self-watering container.

Cucumbers grow straighter on a trellis, and they're less susceptible to mildew. They're also easier to tend and easier to find when you're harvesting.

PICK YOUR POT

Cucumber plants are vines. Even the ones described as "compact" or "semi-bush" are vines. Because they are what they are, cucumber plants will either crawl out of their container to wander through the neighborhood or climb a trellis. For container gardens, the latter is usually the better way to grow cucumbers. Even in an earth garden, trellis-grown cukes take up less room, grow straighter, and are shapelier. They're also easier to tend and harvest.

If you plan to let your cucumber plant roam around as it pleases, use a large container so there's some roaming room. (Expect the plant to wander outside the container anyway.) If you plan to grow your cucumber on a trellis, choose a container that is easy to attach a trellis to.

GROW IT

You can direct-seed cucumbers, but wait until the soil is consistently above 70°F (21°C). In our neck of the woods, temperatures don't reach "cucumber level" until at least a week after the last frost, well into June. To get an earlier crop, we start our own seedlings or purchase plants from a local nursery.

To grow your own transplants, start seeds half an inch deep in four-inch pots about three weeks before transplant date. We start the plants in the same potting soil we use in containers. Sow three seeds to a pot; after germination, snip out the two smallest plants with scissors. Keep temperatures at or above 70°F (21°C) during and after germination. Harden off for about a week before transplanting to a container. When transplanting, be very careful not to disturb the roots; like their squash relatives, cucumbers do not like to be transplanted. If frost threatens, move the container indoors or cover well; cucumber plants cannot survive subfreezing temperatures.

Bug Off

Most of the diseases that afflict cucumbers emerge from garden soil. Because there is no garden soil in your containers, there are virtually no diseases waiting to attack your cucumbers. Late in a hot, damp summer, powdery mildew is sometimes a problem. The best bet is to eliminate the possibility from the beginning by choosing a mildew-resistant variety.

Cucumber beetles, both spotted and striped, plague all members of the squash family, but they are especially partial to their cucumber namesakes. Prevention is the preferred strategy: grow the plants under lightweight row covers so the beetles don't have a chance to set up camp. (Some cucumber varieties, described as nonbitter or bitter-free, are less attractive to cucumber beetles.) If prevention fails, pyrethrin or rotenone will kill the beetles. Be aware, though, that those poisons will also kill any other visitors to the cucumber plant or its flowers — bees, for example, and other pollinating insects.

Eat It

Clip cucumbers from the vine with scissors whenever they are the size you prefer; I think the little ones taste better.

Pick Your Plant

'Boothbay Blonde': an heirloom from Maine; matures to yellow with a mild, sweet flavor

'Diva': an award-winner known for its taste. It also has other qualities that make it a good container vegetable — it's easy to grow, produces only female flowers that don't need to be pollinated to set fruit, is not bitter (and therefore less attractive to cucumber beetles), and is resistant to mildew. The tasty and tender-skinned fruits are best if picked when they are small, about the size of a pickle.

'Little Leaf': a compact plant that will climb a trellis all by itself. It will produce well even if weather is less than the perfect warm, dry, and sunny that cucumbers prefer. 'Little Leaf' sets fruit without pollination. The fruits are classed as "pickling type," but they are tasty in salads too.

'Boothbay Blonde' produces three- to four-inch fruits that turn yellow as they mature.

DANDELION

(*Cichorium intybus*)

This "garden variety" dandelion is not the same plant you'd find in your lawn. Italian dandelion is actually a chicory; it grows faster, larger, and with a deeper green color than a true dandelion, and its flowers are blue, not yellow. The young greens add a sharp, tangy taste to salads, and the mature greens are often braised with bits of bacon and a splash of vinegar.

Italian dandelion is happy to grow in the same container with other salad plants like kale and lettuces.

PICK YOUR POT

Choose a medium or large self-watering container, depending on how many plants you choose to grow. As many as 10 plants will fit in a medium container.

GROW IT

Grow as you would lettuce. If starting plants indoors, sow seeds three or four weeks before the transplant date. Plant two or three about ⅛ inch deep in two-inch cells or in flats, and thin to the strongest plant. Transplant to containers six to eight inches apart. Direct-seed in clusters of two or three seeds every six to eight inches and thin to the strongest plant. Succession plantings every three weeks will ensure a steady supply of greens.

BUG OFF

Nothing appears to bother these tough plants.

EAT IT

The baby plants, at three to five weeks, are less likely to be bitter, and make a nice salad green. Allowed to grow to maturity, the plant can be up to 16 inches tall; at that stage, the leaves are usually cooked rather than eaten raw.

EGGPLANT

(*Solanum melongena*)

If the word eggplant brings to mind only those large, chubby, shiny black fruits that go into eggplant Parmesan, get ready for a consciousness-expanding experience. Eggplants come in all sorts of shapes, sizes, and colors: light pink, deep pink, rose, white, green, and light purple with white stripes. If that's not enough, the fruits are preceded by beautiful flowers. A container gardener with an eye for beauty couldn't ask for more.

PICK YOUR POT

These heat-loving relatives of peppers and tomatoes can be difficult to grow in earth gardens in the cooler areas of the country. But growing eggplants in containers is another story altogether. The same varieties that barely produce in our earth garden thrive in containers; they're one of the plants I now grow *only* in containers. You can grow a single dwarf eggplant in a medium container and up to four in a large container.

GROW IT

Eggplants need to get a head start indoors to produce a crop. If you can get the eggplant seedlings you want at a local nursery or by mail order, do it. If you can't find certain varieties, or if you just like starting your own plants, here's how it's done.

Eggplants are heat lovers, big time. The seeds won't germinate at all in cool soil, and do best between 80 and 90°F (27–32°C). Unless you keep your house that warm all day and night, you'll need to find a consistently warm spot over a radiator — or better yet, invest in a heat mat. After emergence, eggplant seedlings still want a little bottom heat; keep them at about 70°F (21°C).

Eggplants are easily stressed by transplanting, so they do best if started in four-inch pots, where they can grow until they move to their container homes. Eight weeks before the last frost, sow three seeds per pot about ¼ inch deep. Maintain constant soil moisture and temperature. Thin the plants to the strongest one after the true leaves appear. Harden off plants for about a week before transplanting by reducing the temperature to 60°F (15°C) and cutting back on water. Warm the container soil for a few days before transplanting by covering it with black plastic. Eggplants are sensitive not just to frost, but also to cold. They won't be killed by 40°F (4°C) nights, but they will be set back. Growing eggplants under row covers protects them from cool weather.

'Fairy Tale' eggplant produces beautiful flowers and pale purple-striped fruits that are almost too pretty to eat.

The long, thin fruits of this 'Orient Express' are ripe and ready for harvest.

This is less than half the harvest from a container-grown 'Bambino' eggplant.

BUG OFF

Flea beetles are a major pest for eggplants and will defoliate seedlings if given the chance. If you don't protect the plants with row covers, you may have to use a botanical pesticide. Because they are related to potatoes, eggplants are also prey for Colorado potato beetles, which actually seem to prefer eggplants to potato plants. Protect eggplants the same way you would potato plants: handpick any adult beetle you find and check the undersides of leaves for the bright orange egg clusters the adults have probably laid. Check daily for adult and larval beetles. If things really get out of control, use the Bt strain that kills Colorado potato beetle larvae (*Bacillus thuringiensis* var. *tenebrionis*).

EAT IT

Harvest the fruits with scissors to avoid damaging the plant. The fruits taste best when harvested at a stage that the plant deems immature, about half the size of the mature fruit. This "early" harvest also stimulates further fruit production. With a heavy crop of fruit, the plants may need staking or some similar form of support.

PICK YOUR PLANT

Eggplants are available in short-and-plump as well as long-and-skinny forms and in many colors. They all taste good, but some are — to my eye — more attractive than others. I'll admit I let my eyes make the choice sometimes. The smaller-fruited varieties have the reputation of being easier to grow.

'**Bambino**': round, 1½-inch fruits on a compact, 12-inch plant; bears early compared to other eggplants

'**Fairy Tale**': tender, long, and purple striped, with a compact plant and fruits that grow in clusters

'**Neon**': bears deep pink fruits that fall about halfway between short-and-plump and long-and-skinny; fairly described in one seed catalog as an "edible work of art"

'**Orient Express**': Asian-style long, thin black fruits

ENDIVE AND ESCAROLE

(Cichorium endivia)

These members of the chicory family are the same yet different. They're genetically the same plant, but endive has curly leaves, while escarole's are not so frilly and have a milder taste. Both are easy to grow and a nice addition to a salad in any season. Young leaves are more tender and not as pungent.

PICK YOUR POT

These plants thrive in self-watering containers. Any container that will grow lettuce will grow escarole and endive — from a window box to a large container.

GROW IT

Grow as you would lettuce, either in cells for transplanting or by direct seeding. Plant two or three seeds, ⅛ inch deep, in each two-inch cell. Direct seeding can start in early spring and continue throughout the gardening season — sow in groups of two or three seeds, 8–10 inches apart. (If you plan to harvest as baby greens or cut-and-come-again, sow thickly in a band with seeds an inch apart.) Thin to the strongest plant in each cluster.

Some diners like the taste of endive better if it is blanched. Tie the leaves together and cover with a plate or pot — anything to block sunlight. These are hardy plants whose flavor is improved by a few frosts; they'll go on producing into early winter with a little protection using a row cover.

BUG OFF

Neither endive nor escarole has any garden enemies of note.

EAT IT

Pick outer leaves as soon as they're big enough to use or wait and harvest the whole plant. Or, if you want baby greens, clip the thickly sown plants when they are about four inches long.

PICK YOUR PLANT

'**Bianca Riccia**': light green endive; a good choice for close planting; harvest as baby greens for salads; hardy

'**Nataly**': dark green escarole; self-blanching; heat tolerant

'**Neos**': dark green, very frilly endive; self-blanching; better in cool weather than in the heat of summer

'Bianca Riccia' endive is easy to grow in self-watering containers, and is a fine addition to salads. Belgian endive (below) is blanched for tenderness and sweeter flavor.

GARLIC

(*Allium sativum*)

When I think of garlic, I think of dried and cured cloves in a papery husk. Green garlic is something else entirely — it's the young garlic shoot, the first part of the plant to emerge after the clove sprouts and starts to become a plant. It has a milder taste than that of garlic cloves, but it can be used in any dish where the taste of garlic would be welcome. It's also easy to plant, and perfectly suited to life in a container.

This is green garlic at harvesttime. Just wash, trim the roots, and eat as you would scallions.

Like regular bulbs of garlic, green garlic is planted from cloves. Be sure to plant with the pointy end up!

PICK YOUR POT

Any self-watering container with at least six inches of soil depth can be used for growing green garlic. Plant it in among other vegetables as a crop to be harvested before its partners need all the growing room in the container.

GROW IT

It couldn't be easier. Separate the cloves from a head of garlic, leaving on the husk. Punch a hole in the soil with a finger and insert the clove, pointy end up. That's it.

PESTS AND DISEASE

I have yet to find garlic bothered by any sort of garden pest, large or small.

EAT IT

There are two choices. After the leaves have started to form, about four to five weeks after planting, pull the plants and trim away the roots. The rest of the plant, including the small bulb, can be eaten — added to soups, salsas, stir-fries, and pestos or grilled as a side dish for barbecued meats. The second choice is to harvest just foliage, leaf by leaf, about an inch above the soil. It will regrow four or five times before all the energy in the bulb is used up.

PICK YOUR PLANT

Any of the many varieties of garlic will produce good green garlic, but we've had good luck with the following.

'German Extra Hardy': a vigorous grower with red clove skin and a strong, pungent flavor

KALE

(*Brassica oleracea*, Acephala Group)

If you had to design the perfect container vegetable, you might well end up with kale. All of its many versions are attractive plants with bold color and texture. It's easy to grow, rarely bothered by pests, and chock-full of nutrients. Perhaps best of all, kale produces far into the frosty days of winter; its flavor is improved after it has weathered a few frosts.

PICK YOUR POT

Grow up to 24 plants in a large, self-watering container or as part of a mixed salad garden.

GROW IT

For a salad mix, sow thickly and harvest the leaves when they are still young and tender, at four weeks or so. For a season-long crop, sow seeds in groups of three, ¼–½ inch deep, with the groups about eight inches apart. After emergence, thin with scissors to one plant per group. Kale plants can become fairly large (two feet or more) and may need supplemental feeding during the season with liquid seaweed fertilizer.

BUG OFF

Although not as favored by pests as many of its cabbage-family cousins, kale does play host to aphids and flea beetles, especially when the plants are young and tender.

Check the plants carefully for aphids at transplanting. Grow kale under row covers to protect against flea beetles.

HARVEST

Clip young leaves at four or five weeks old or let the plant grow for a couple of months and harvest larger leaves, letting the smaller ones remain for later harvest.

PICK YOUR PLANT

'**Red Russian**': the stems qualify as reddish purple, the leaves are blue-green; tender and good in salads

'**Toscano**': also known as 'Lacinato' or dinosaur kale; it is dark green and full of vitamins

'**Wild Red**': beautiful, hardy, and tasty, which ornamental kales often are not

'**Winterbor**': very hardy; withstands hard frosts below 20°F

'Wild Red' kale is as decorative as it is tasty and productive.

The crinkly leaves of 'Winterbor' are sweetened by frost.

KOHLRABI

(*Brassica oleracea*, Gongylodes Group)

Kohlrabi is from the cabbage family, but it sure doesn't take after any of its relatives; it looks more like an alien spacecraft than it does a vegetable. But it is a vegetable, and a tasty one at that. It's easy to grow, not bothered by pests, and thrives in the rich, moist soil of a container. The white flesh tastes something like broccoli, and is used raw in salads and slaws, in many cooked dishes, and just for munching.

'Winner' kohlrabi looks like a spaceship but tastes like broccoli — outta this world!

PICK YOUR POT

Grow nine plants in a large self-watering container.

GROW IT

Kohlrabi does best in cool weather. In the North, that means spring planting starting a month or so before the last frost; in warmer climates, start in late fall for a winter crop or late winter for a spring harvest. Kohlrabi can be started in flats and transplanted, but is easiest to grow direct-seeded. Sow two or three seeds in clusters six inches apart and thin to one plant with scissors after emergence.

BUG OFF

Like other brassicas, kohlrabi is sometimes bothered by flea beetles. Protect young plants with a row cover.

EAT IT

Harvest kohlrabi when the bulbous stems are two inches in diameter. If plants are allowed to mature, the tough outer skin of the bulb may need to be peeled before eating.

PICK YOUR PLANT

'Kolibi': purple/red on the outside and white on the inside

'Winner': a light green variety noted for its improved taste

LEEKS

(Allium ampeloprasum)

Like their allium cousins garlic and onions, leeks have to make it through life with a fairly small root system supporting a fairly substantial amount of plant material. Therefore, like garlic and onions, leeks need convenient access to plenty of food and water, and freedom from competition with any other plants. All of that is easy to provide in a self-watering container filled with a compost-based growing medium. In addition to plenty of food and water, leeks need as much time as they can get to bask in the sun.

PICK YOUR POT

I like to grow leeks in a large self-watering container at least 8 inches deep, which provides enough space for 8 to 10 plants. Grow leeks alone; they don't compete well with other plants.

GROW IT

If you live where the growing season includes at least three months of warm and sunny weather, you may be able to grow leeks from seed outdoors, but most gardeners are better off with transplants. I'm fortunate to have a local nursery that sells them, so I buy the dozen or so plants I need for less than half the cost of a packet of seeds.

To grow your own transplants, sow seeds in a flat in late winter. When the plants are large enough to handle, transplant to small (one-and-one-half inch) cells in the same soil that you'll use in containers. Keep them well watered, and fertilize as necessary. (Plants grown in the soil mix described on page 36 may not need additional fertilizer, but a dose of liquid seaweed fertilizer every three weeks or so won't hurt.)

Plant leeks outdoors in late spring about a week after the last frost. Keep the container reservoir full and fertilize every month or so. Make a hole with a dowel or pencil about four inches deep and drop in the leek plant.

For the best leeks with the longest edible stems, add more soil two or three times during the growing period, finally hilling the plants somewhat above the container sides.

Healthy leek foliage like this 'King Richard' will feed the growth of a long white root hidden beneath the soil.

HILLING LEEKS

Although their strappy blue-green foliage is quite attractive, the best part of a leek is what lies beneath the soil. The long, white base of the plant is what you actually eat, and the more of it there is, the better.

To get the most from your leeks, you need to hill them — that is, bury the base of the plants with soil as they grow, to keep them from turning green and to produce longer, whiter plants. You'll end up with a mounded container by the end of the season, but if you're using a self-watering container, the soil will always stay moist to the surface.

BUG OFF

Like my other alliums, the leeks I've planted haven't been bothered by pests, and I have not yet found them susceptible to any disease.

EAT IT

Although leeks can withstand a *light* frost, you should harvest them (or move the container indoors) before a hard frost threatens. Leeks will keep for a couple of weeks in the refrigerator, but they're better eaten fresh.

PICK YOUR PLANT

'**King Richard**': white stems with medium green leaves. Tolerates light frosts

'**Lincoln**': a miniature variety grown from seed. Sow thickly and harvest when the plants are about finger-size.

LETTUCE

(*Lactuca sativa*)

*L*ettuce? No, what we're really talking about here is lettuces. Many, many different kinds, colors, sizes, textures, and tastes of lettuces. And, although they are commonly referred to as "salad greens," they are not all green, and even those that are green sport different shades of that color. Lettuces in a container garden are a feast for both the palette and the palate; they're both beautiful and tasty.

PICK YOUR POT

Lettuce is a container plant par excellence. Since we started experimenting with container gardening, we've grown very little of our lettuce in our earth garden. We've found that lettuce grows just as well or better in containers, and it's ever so handy to have salad greens growing right on the porch.

Lettuces are easy to grow, provided you're very attentive to their two needs — constant moisture and moderate temperatures. Both of these needs are easier to meet in self-watering containers than in traditional pots or in the earth garden.

A short period of dry soil will not kill a lettuce plant, but it will affect its taste, introducing a bitterness that subsequent watering will not remove. This quality, which makes growing the very best-tasting lettuce in either traditional containers or in the earth garden difficult, makes lettuce a first-class choice for self-watering containers. They're never lacking water, and also never flooded with too much.

Because their root systems are not very big, lettuces are quite content to grow in containers most other vegetable plants would find too confining. We've had very good results with self-watering window boxes, and we've even grown 'Tom Thumb' in self-watering hanging planters. Bigger containers also work fine, but I've found that a series of plantings in smaller containers can easily keep us in salad greens through the summer.

GROW IT

I start lettuce depending on how I plan to harvest it. If I'm going to harvest leaf by leaf or cut-and-come-again, I want a dense planting — pretty much a solid mass of greenery. To get that result, I direct-seed, broadcasting to achieve a coverage of a seed every ½ inch or so. I use the mixes offered in many seed catalogs, to get a variety of colors, textures, and tastes.

These lettuces from a salad mix are spaced fairly close together; I'll harvest whole plants at about this stage.

Lettuce seeds are very small, so they should be close to the soil surface, just barely covered with fine-textured planting mix. (Crumble the soil between your palms to break up any clumps. The objective is to keep the seeds in contact with soil particles and therefore with the water held by those particles.) The keys to good germination are: moderate temperatures — no higher than 60°F (15°C); and moisture all the time — not ever sopping wet, but also never dry.

If I want mature lettuce plants instead of baby greens, I start the seeds in flats and transplant them into containers when the leaves are two or three inches long. I use this method with the butterhead or bibb lettuces that form loose heads. 'Tom Thumb' is our favorite for containers; the heads are about the right size for an individual salad. Six or eight of them will fit in a small hanging container, and quite a few more in a window box.

This 'Black-Seeded Simpson' and 'Red Salad Bowl' were given plenty of room to grow and produce full-size heads.

My favorite way to grow salad greens — a self-watering window box filled with lettuce mix, red kale, 'Bright Lights' chard, arugula, and Johnny-Jump-Ups.

BUG OFF

In theory, lettuce is host to a few pests, notably aphids and flea beetles. In practice, the aphids and flea beetles in my garden prefer other plants and cause little or no damage to the lettuces.

EAT IT

You can take your pick on when to pick your lettuce. Just snip off the leaves one by one as soon as they reach the size you want. This works for any except the iceberg types, and is especially good for leaf lettuces.

Cut the whole plant an inch or more above the soil. It will regrow once, and sometimes twice. This is the best method for leaf types planted close together. (Try a mix of different colors and textures in one container.) Harvest the whole plant when the head is mature but still young and tender.

PICK YOUR PLANT

Lettuces are generally grouped by seed merchants as leaf, romaine or cos, butterhead or bibb, and summer crisp.

LEAF LETTUCES

These don't form a head but instead grow as a loose rosette from which you can pick the outer leaves as they reach the size you want. These lettuces are also good candidates for cut-and-come-again harvesting, where you cut the whole plant an inch above the soil and let it grow a new set of leaves.

'Berenice': a green oak leaf with improved heat tolerance

'Black-Seeded Simpson': an old-timer that never wears out its welcome; quick to produce a crop; moderately heat tolerant; crisp and tasty

'Red Sails': a knock-your-socks-off beautiful plant with fringed and ruffled leaves with a light green center and brilliant burgundy-red edges; crisp texture with a mild taste and very good bolt resistance

'Red Salad Bowl': a burgundy-red oak leaf with deeply lobed leaves; good bolt resistance

ROMAINE LETTUCES

These have a more upright habit than other lettuces, with long leaves that grow into a tighter bunch as a plant matures.

'Freckles': bright green leaves with red spots; beautiful in a container or a salad bowl; good as baby greens or left to form a gorgeous head at maturity

'Winter Density': dark green with a shape somewhere between a classic romaine and a bibb; excellent salad lettuce with considerable frost tolerance

BUTTERHEAD LETTUCES

These are our favorites for taste and texture. We usually let these lettuces grow until they form a head rather than harvesting them leaf by leaf.

'Buttercrunch': perfectly named; matures as a six-inch head with dark green outer leaves and a blanched yellow center

'Deer Tongue': an heirloom lettuce with smooth, tongue-shaped leaves

'Tom Thumb': the perfect container lettuce; forms small heads just right for an individual salad, and you can grow a half dozen of them in a small hanging container. The only problem is that they're so cute growing that I can't bear to eat them.

SUMMER CRISP VARIETIES

These are fairly heat tolerant, sweet, and juicy. They begin life like leaf lettuces, but mature with a compact head.

'Loma': crunchy like iceberg, but tasty; compact heads suitable for smaller containers

'Magenta': red-tinged leaves with good heat tolerance

MESCLUN

Mesclun isn't a vegetable; it's a whole bunch of vegetables. The word means "mixture" in French, and it refers to a whole bunch of mixes of a whole bunch of vegetables. The common denominator is that all the mixes are meant to end up in a salad bowl. Seed catalogs often feature as many as six or eight custom mesclun mixes of various garden greens that taste good together. Some mesclun mixes are all lettuces; some have no lettuce at all.

Other greens (though they are not all green) that appear in mesclun mixes are mizuna, purslane, orach, chervil, mâche, arugula, endive, fennel, chives, dill, parsley, chicory, cress, radicchio, mustard, and dandelion. And there's no rule that you can't make up your own. As long as it's a mixture, it's mesclun.

Direct-sow mesclun, aiming for close spacing for a cut-and-come-again harvest. (Shake the seeds in their packet to ensure that they are well mixed before you plant.) Harvest as "baby greens" at about three weeks, when the plants are three to four inches tall. Cut with scissors about ½ inch above the soil.

MÂCHE

(*Valerianella locusta*)

Mâche is a miniature cool-weather gourmet salad green that is a natural for containers Also known as corn salad and lamb's lettuce and very popular in Europe, it is just beginning to gain a following in this country. Mâche prefers cool weather and is remarkably hardy — a sure bet for early-spring gardens.

The tender leaves of mâche make an excellent early-spring salad.

PICK YOUR POT

Any self-watering container that can grow lettuce will grow mâche. That's pretty much any container, with the size depending on how much you want to grow.

GROW IT

Mâche will grow well in relatively shallow containers such as window boxes. Direct-sow in the early spring, ¼–½ inch deep and about one inch apart. When the plants begin to crowd one another, thin to two inches apart and use the thinnings in salad. For fall and winter harvest, plant in late August or early September. Mâche is very hardy and will keep producing well into frosty weather if protected by a row cover or an unheated greenhouse. Because mâche tastes better when young, you're better off with a series of small plantings two weeks apart than with a single larger planting.

BUG OFF

Pests and disease do not appear to be a problem.

EAT IT

Harvest whole plants when still young and before daytime temperatures exceed the 60–70°F (15–21°C) range. Mâche doesn't bolt easily, but its flavor declines in warm weather.

PICK YOUR PLANT

'Verte de Cambral': small leaves and very hardy

'Large-Leaf Round': a good choice for spring planting for an early-summer harvest

MUSTARD

(*Brassica juncea*)

*M*ustard greens are hot and zesty when eaten raw in salads but milder and mellow when cooked. Either way, they're a healthful addition to any container garden. Like many other salad greens, mustard comes in different colors, adding visual delights to their culinary ones.

PICK YOUR POT

Choose the container based on how much mustard you want to grow and whether you're sowing seeds thickly to harvest young salad greens or allowing individual plants to mature for braising greens.

GROW IT

Direct-sow starting in early spring with succession plantings every two or three weeks until late summer. Mustard is not at its best in warm weather (it doesn't germinate well or taste as good), so skip summer plantings and resume in the early fall.

EAT IT

Begin the harvest when the plant has formed a rosette of leaves; from that point onward, pick individual leaves that are three to four inches long. Or wait until the plants are about six inches tall, then harvest the whole plant.

BUG OFF

Pests and diseases do not appear to be a problem.

PICK YOUR PLANT

'**Green Wave**': bright green, curly leaves; reaches "baby green" size in three weeks and matures in 40 days

'**Osaka Purple**': from Japan; medium green leaves with purple-red veins

'**Red Giant**': a Japanese heirloom with purple-tinted leaves and a peppery taste; often used in spicy mesclun mixes; the purple is more intense in cool temperatures

These seedlings of 'Red Giant' are spaced about right for harvest as braising greens in a few weeks.

This 'Green Wave' mustard is ready to be picked for a salad.

ONIONS

(*Allium cepa*)

If you give an onion what it wants by way of water and food, it will ask very little else of you. Onions are rarely bothered by pests and are prone to few diseases; they therefore require very little tending. But they must grow in rich, moist soil, and they don't like competition from other plants; their small root system makes them easy to overwhelm. Fortunately, it's a simple matter to give onions a good life in a self-watering container.

A large self-watering container can grow 18 onions, half a dozen each of white, yellow, and red, grown from sets.

The onion's root system is fairly small for the plant it needs to nourish. Because of this, onions don't compete well with other plants, and are best grown by themselves.

PICK YOUR POT

I grow onions all by themselves in a large, self-watering container, putting in as many as 18 plants per container.

GROW IT

You get three choices for getting started with onions: 1) start from seeds, either indoors or outdoors; 2) start with plants; or 3) start with sets. If you have a long, frost-free growing season of at least three months and a sunny, warm location, you can direct-sow onions. If your conditions are less than prime, you'll be better off either starting your own plants indoors or buying started plants. If you start with sets (tiny onion bulbs), you're pretty much guaranteed to have a crop, but onion experts generally say that set-grown onions don't grow quite as well as seed-grown onions. You will, at any rate, find more varieties available as seeds than as sets.

Direct-sow onions when the soil temperature is at least 50°F (10°C). Sow two or three seeds at one-inch intervals at about ⅜ inch deep. When the plants are about two inches tall, thin to one plant per cluster by clipping the extra plants with scissors. When the plants reach four inches or so, thin again to two inches apart for a larger number of smaller onions or to four inches apart for larger onions. Pull the extra plants this time and either transplant them or toss them into a salad or soup.

To start onion plants from seed, begin in late winter. (We get them going in late February in Vermont.) Sow in a flat about ½ inch apart or plant four or five seeds per cell. Whenever the onion tops grow long enough to droop a bit (five to six inches), treat them to a "haircut." Clip back the tops to about three inches to stimulate root growth. Transplant to containers (spaced as recommended above) about a month before the last frost date. I usually give the onions one last haircut a few days before transplanting. (Just dig up a clump of plants and separate them gently; onions can tolerate the kind of rough handling that would kill any other plant.)

Warning! Purchased onion plants, especially those you get by mail, may look terrible. In fact, they may look dead. But they're not; they'll perk up and grow just fine. I've seen it with my own eyes, and I wouldn't have believed it otherwise. Plant the onions as soon as you can after they arrive, spacing them as recommended above. (Purchased plants also seem to benefit from a "haircut" before they are planted. There is less plant for the disturbed roots to support.)

Plant onion sets so that the tips are right at soil level. Space as recommended above. (It's a bit counterintuitive, but small sets — about the size of a dime — are less likely to bolt than big sets.) Onion sets are reputed to be more prone to disease than onions grown from seed. I've not encountered any problems, but to be on the safe side, I make a habit of not mixing sets and plants in the same container.

BUG OFF

I have yet to encounter an onion with any sort of disease, and none of the pests in my container garden will have anything to do with an onion.

EAT IT

Onions can be harvested at any stage of growth, from early thinnings, to "green" onions about an inch in diameter, to mature onions that can be as big as four inches across. Onions are finished growing when the tops begin to flop over. They should be harvested then; they don't improve by sitting in the soil after that point. The onions we grow in containers are all for fresh eating and are usually sweet onions that aren't meant to store for more than a few weeks. If you grow onions for storage, cure them in the sun for about a week, until the tops are dry and the outer skin of the bulbs is dry and crinkly.

The best onion sets are about the size of a dime.

DAY LENGTH MATTERS

Onions come in two versions — long-day and short-day. Long-day onions need about 14 hours of daylight to stimulate bulb formation; they grow best in the North. Short-day onions form bulbs when they have about equal amounts of day and night; they grow best in the South.

PICK YOUR PLANT

'**Olympic**': easy to grow from seed; matures early

'**Stuttgarter**': the best onion to grow from sets; stores well

'**Walla Walla**': a large, sweet onion; best used fresh

ORACH

(*Atriplex hortensis*)

Also known as mountain spinach, orach comes in green, golden, and magenta varieties. Frost sensitive as a seedling, orach prefers to start growing outdoors only when all danger of frost is past. At maturity, it can tolerate a few degrees of frost and go on producing for colorful salads and cooked greens into the late fall. It tastes quite a lot like spinach, especially when eaten steamed.

Most of these red orach leaves are still salad size, but a few have reached the point where they're best eaten steamed.

PICK YOUR POT

Orach is a big plant, reaching five feet (if you allow it). Plan to grow it in a large self-watering container all on its own.

GROW IT

Direct-sow ¼ inch deep in early summer. Expect the first harvest of leaves in about six weeks. Prune the growing tips with scissors to control height and shape, and to encourage the growth of new leaves.

BUG OFF

Orach seems to be free of disease and of no interest to pests.

EAT IT

Start harvesting leaves when they are an inch or so long for salad or about four inches for steaming. Or cut the whole plant when it is about six inches tall.

PICK YOUR PLANT

'Aureus': yellow-gold leaves and a mild flavor

'Green Spires': a green orach with a slightly sweet flavor

'Rubra': red orach with a flavor like spinach

Pak Choi

(*Brassica rapa,* Chinensis Group)

Pak choi, pac choi, and bok choy are not different vegetables, just different spellings of the same vegetable. However you spell it, pak choi is easy to grow, especially in containers. Like all of its brassica cousins, pak choi has a relatively compact root system growing close to the soil surface. Hence, it thrives in a nutrient-rich soil that never dries out — just what it gets in a self-watering container filled with a compost-rich potting soil.

PICK YOUR POT

Pak choi will grow in any size self-watering container; I put in eight plants per large container.

GROW IT

You can direct-sow pak choi, but we prefer to start it indoors, two or three seeds to a cell. When the seedlings have emerged, thin to the best plant by cutting the rest at the soil line with scissors. For a spring crop, direct-sow two weeks before the last frost; for a fall crop, sow in late July or early August.

BUG OFF

Like its Oriental and domestic cabbage cousins, pak choi is beloved by flea beetles, especially when the plants are young and tender. Protect the seedlings with row covers, or refer to chapter nine for more pest-control options.

EAT IT

Harvest the whole plant by cutting at soil level.

PICK YOUR PLANT

Chinese pak choi: very easy to grow; about 16 inches high; and bolt resistant

'Mei Qing' choi: a baby pak choi about six inches high at maturity; easy to grow; bolt resistant; well suited to containers

Off to a good start, this 'Mei Qing' choi will soon be ready to harvest.

PEAS

(*Pisum sativum*)

Although they're not generally thought of this way, peas are a multipurpose vegetable — the pretty blossoms are edible, as are the tendrils that pea plants use to help them climb trellises. Shelling peas are grown for the nascent pea seeds inside the pods. Sugar snap peas have edible pods filled with edible peas. Snow peas are grown for their pods, with barely developed little peas inside.

Although the vines of 'Dakota' are described in catalogs as "medium-short," they still grow better if given some support.

PICK YOUR POT

It takes quite a few pea plants to produce a meal of peas; grow them in a large self-watering container, preferably one that is easy to equip with a trellis. Plant peas closely (½ inch apart) on both sides of the trellis, and you can get 50 or 60 plants in a large container.

GROW IT

Seed catalogs list some short pea varieties that — according to the descriptions — do not need a trellis. I have not found that to be the case. Peas, even the ones with "short" vines, grow better and are much easier to harvest if given a support of some kind.

Giving plants vertical support in a container, however, is more challenging than it is in an earth garden. In most cases, the container soil is neither deep enough nor firm enough to support a trellis. Some containers are designed to be equipped with an accessory trellis, but you can also create your own.

Place a post outside the container at both ends, and anchor them either by driving them into the ground or by attaching them to a stabilizing crosspiece. Attach another crosspiece to the top and attach chicken wire or plastic netting to the uprights and the top. If you want more room for peas, make the top crosspiece long enough that there's room for two or more containers beneath it.

Peas like cool weather, so plant the seeds early in the spring, after inoculating them with nitrogen-fixing rhizobia (see page 146). Sow the seeds about an inch deep and ½ inch apart. Use a staggered pattern, as shown at right, with at least two rows of seeds on either side of the trellis. The object is to get as many pea plants as possible growing as near as possible to the trellis.

As the peas grow, they'll reach out and grasp the trellis with tendrils. Usually. Occasionally they appear to become confused;

if this happens, lead then gently back where they're supposed to be. I've found that peas are more likely to grab chicken wire than plastic netting. If the vines begin to pull away from the trellis and bulge outward, loop some garden twine around the whole mass and gently snug it back against the netting.

Bug Off

Most pea diseases are soilborne and therefore not likely to be a problem for container-grown plants. Powdery mildew can be avoided by growing resistant varieties.

Eat It

The harvest rules for peas are pretty simple: pick 'em often and pick 'em all. Don't pick peas when the vines are wet. Do use two hands — holding a vine with one hand, pull the pea pod loose with the other. Most shelling pea varieties are at peak sugar stage for just a short time. Before and after the peak, the taste won't be the same.

How can I tell from the look and feel of the pea pod if the peas inside are perfectly ripe? I experiment. (And I have a good time doing it.) Pick a pea pod that looks full but not too full and feels as if the peas inside are plump but not too big. Open the pod and taste the peas. Continue the experiment until you are consistently picking perfectly ripe peas. This may take a while, but you won't mind. Different pea varieties may feel or look different when ripe, so you'll have to conduct the experiment all over again if you grow more than one variety. Once you've defined *ripe*, pick everything that's ripe; if any pods stay on the vine and grow peas to the tasteless, starchy seed stage that the plant wants, the plant will think it has accomplished its mission and stop making more blossoms and more pea pods.

Sugar peas should have plump pods that snap the way a snap bean does. (To be sure, though, always taste-test. Like shelling peas, snap peas are very tasty raw.) Some sugar snap peas have strings, like string beans; before you eat them, break off the tip of the pod, where it's attached to the plant, and pull the string from the pod. Snow peas taste best when they are of medium size, before the peas inside have developed very much.

Plant peas about ½ inch apart in double rows on each side of a trellis. It takes a lot of plants to get a good harvest.

Pick Your Plant

I tend to favor smaller pea plants in containers because they need smaller trellises.

SHELLING PEAS

'Dakota': extra early, on medium-short vines

'Eclipse': medium-short, three-foot vines; stays sweet longer on the vine than others

SNAP PEAS

'Sugar Ann': short (two-foot) vines

'Sugar Sprint': short vines and stringless

SNOW PEAS

'Snow Green': short vines and sweet flavor

PEPPERS

(*Capsicum annuum*)

Peppers are a feast for the eyes as well as for the tongue. If you're used to garden-variety green peppers, get ready for some surprises. Sweet peppers come in yellow, orange, and chocolate brown. Some chili pepper varieties display on one plant fruits at different colorful stages of ripeness — purple, yellow, orange, and red. Peppers are as varied in taste as they are in color, ranging from sweet and mild to raging hot; they can be eaten raw, cooked, dried, powdered. They are an artistic, horticultural, and culinary adventure.

'Chilly Chili' has all the visual appeal of a regular chili pepper with none of the heat.

PICK YOUR POT

Because they love heat and consistent moisture, pepper plants are especially well suited to self-watering containers. Many varieties are compact enough to do well in medium containers or to mix with other small plants in a large container.

GROW IT

Once they're up and growing, peppers are easy keepers that require little attention. But getting them to that stage can be a challenge; much of their fuss has to do with temperature.

Like their eggplant cousins, peppers are heat lovers, especially during germination. They won't bother to germinate in cool soil (below 65°F [18°C]) and do best at soil temperatures between 80 and 90°C (27–32°C). If the soil gets below 80°F (27°C), pepper seeds germinate at a lower and slower rate. Slow germination stresses plants; they start life behind the eight ball and never catch up. Unless you live in a sauna, you'll need to place your seed trays on a heat mat to provide this kind of temperature range. Sow two or three seeds per cell, ¼ inch deep, eight weeks before transplanting outdoors. Keep the soil moist. When the first true leaves appear, transplant to four-inch pots. Now you have a choice. Your peppers will grow and produce fairly well if you keep them at about 70°F (21°C) during the day and 60°F (15°C) at night. But they'll produce more blossoms and set more fruit if, when the third set of true leaves appears, you lower the nighttime temperature to about 55°F (13°C) for four weeks. Continue to provide 70°F (21°C) daytime temperatures and full sun. (Peppers can do with even more than full sun; if you have a grow light, they will appreciate up to 16 hours of light a day.)

Transplant your peppers only after all danger of frost is past and the soil is dependably warm (at least 70°F [21°C]). Set plants about a foot apart. Peppers benefit from the extra warmth of a row cover, but remove the cover when blossoms appear.

Once they start producing fruits, pepper plants have a lot of work to do; and they need a good root system to support that work. Early in its life, keep the plant's attention focused on that root system and not on blossoms and fruit. Prune any blossoms that appear before transplanting outdoors or within a couple of weeks after transplanting. Your harvest will be a bit later but substantially larger.

Bug Off

Peppers are generally healthy when grown in a fertile container soil and do not attract many pests. Aphids and flea beetles may appear on the plants, but usually find other plants more to their liking.

Eat It

Clip green peppers when they are of a size to suit you. Fully ripe peppers (no longer green) are sweeter.

Pick Your Plant

'Ace': dependable, productive red bell pepper

'Chilly Chili': a mild-flavored and very colorful chili on an attractive, compact plant

'Islander': ripens through stages of violet, yellow, and orange streaks to deep red

'Jingle Bells': a compact plant with an upright growth habit

'Numex Twilight': a colorful pepper that starts off purple, then moves through all the colors of a sunset, from yellow to orange and finally red

'Sweet Chocolate': early bell pepper that ripens to dark brown

A perfect container pepper plant, 'Jingle Bells', is compact and produces a crop of beautiful two-inch fruits.

Fans of hot peppers will want to grow 'Numex Twilight' for dinner. I grow it as a feast for the eyes.

POTATOES

(Solanum tuberosum)

Raising enough potatoes to last the winter takes a lot of space. But new potatoes are a whole different chapter in the potato saga. New potatoes are not a different kind of spud; they're the same varieties I could grow in my earth garden, but are harvested much earlier. I can think of few edibles that can compare with a bowl of the first new potatoes and the last fresh peas.

This is only part of the harvest from a half-dozen 'Russian Banana' potato plants.

CONTAINER SELECTION

Potatoes like a rich, slightly acid soil and a constant supply of water; stop-and-go watering is as bad for potatoes as stop-and-go driving is for automobiles. Potatoes have one other need, almost a peculiarity: they're much more productive if they are grown with part of their stem buried. In the earth garden, we accomplish this by "hilling," periodically mounding the soil up around the emerging potato plant and burying about half of the part that had been above the soil surface. Potato tubers grow from the buried stem, between the planted "seed potato" and the soil surface. To pull off this trick in a container, start with a deep (12-inch) container at least 12 inches wide.

GROW IT

Plant potatoes in the late spring; they can tolerate light frost and grow in cool soil. Put about five inches of container soil in the container, then the "seed potatoes," about four inches apart and four inches in from the container sides. Add another two inches of soil. Plants should emerge in two or three weeks. When the plants are six inches high, add enough soil to bury them about halfway. Do it again when the plants have grown again to six inches high, filling the container right to the top. Add more soil when the plants grow another few inches, this time forming a mound that is higher than the container sides. Make sure there is always water in the reservoir. Restrain yourself until the new potatoes are big enough to harvest.

BUG OFF

The main potato pest, the Colorado potato beetle, was named after its host. Although there are ways to poison these pests, I've never had a problem keeping them under control by hand-picking. (Refer to chapter nine.)

EAT IT

This part is just plain fun — a treasure hunt. After about two months, or when some potato flowers appear, or when you just can't hold back any longer, dig right down with a hand, close by the plant stem, and feel around gently until you find a potato big enough to eat. Keep feeling and finding until you get enough for dinner. At the end of the season, remove the soil, sifting through it as you go, to reap the last of the harvest, any potatoes you missed earlier.

The time of harvest for new potatoes is quite a bit earlier, long before the plants die back and signal that the tubers underground have grown as much as they're going to. New potatoes are ready as soon as they're big enough to bother with — generally about two months after planting. (If the variety you're growing is one that flowers, the spuds are ready when the blossoms appear.) What you'll harvest are fairly small, very tender tubers with thin skin. They wouldn't, if given the chance, store well, but they're not meant for storage.

PICK YOUR PLANT

The best potatoes for storing and baking are not always the best new potatoes, which are steamed or boiled rather than baked. In a new potato, "waxy texture" is a quality to look for in catalog descriptions. A potato that is described as good for boiling or for potato salad is a good bet as a new potato. I like to grow the tiny fingerling types that are rarely available in stores.

'Rose Finn Apple': a fingerling with red to pink skin over creamy yellow flesh; white flowers

'Russian Banana': a fingerling with yellow flesh that holds up well when boiled; lavender flowers

'Yukon Gold': my favorite full-size potato, with light yellow flesh and yellowish skin; violet flowers

WHEN A SEED IS NOT A SEED

Unlike most garden plants, potatoes grow not from seed, but from last year's potatoes (or at least a piece of them). To grow a potato, start with a potato. Or, if the spud is larger than a couple of inches in diameter, cut it into two or more pieces, each containing at least one *eye*. (The eye is a depression from which a sprout grows to produce the potato plant stem.) Let the cut pieces dry for a day and then plant them.

Fill the bottom of a large, deep container with soil. Lay half a dozen seed potatoes (or seed potato pieces) on it, and cover them with two or three inches of soil. As the potato stems grow, "hill" them by adding more soil in mounds around the base of each plant.

PUMPKIN

(*Cucurbita pepo*)

Pumpkins may not be the first vegetable you'd think about growing in a container, if only because of their size. I've grown pumpkins in the garden that are bigger than some of my containers. But not all pumpkins are huge, and we've had good luck growing miniature pumpkins in containers. These pumpkins are small, but aside from that, they make very good pies and kid-pleasing jack-o'-lanterns. The cultivar 'Baby Bear' even has semi-hull-less seeds that you can roast and eat.

This 'Baby Bear' pumpkin is ready for harvest and a future as a tiny jack-o'-lantern or a pie.

PICK YOUR POT

The vines do like to escape from the container and run along the ground, but these plants get all the food and water they need to produce attractive fruits in a large self-watering container. Plant one pumpkin per container.

GROW IT

Direct-sow after danger of frost is past, or start seeds indoors three weeks before the last frost date.

BUG OFF

Young plants can be damaged by cucumber beetles; row covers will protect against the pests and provide some additional warmth to hasten growth.

EAT IT

Cut the stem close to the vine. Harvest before a hard frost; cover to protect against light frosts.

PICK YOUR PLANT

'Baby Bear': our favorite mini pumpkin, with a nice, deep orange color; a good pie pumpkin, keeps very well; and spineless stems make it easy for children to handle

'Jack Be Little': a bit flatter in shape and a bit larger in diameter than 'Wee-B-Little'; sweet flesh

'Wee-B-Little': the smallest of the small pumpkins, averaging three inches in diameter; semi-bush growth habit doesn't spread as far as the types that grow as vines

RADICCHIO

(*Cichorium intybus*)

*R*adicchio is a salad green used often in Italian cooking; it is a chicory, a close kin to endive and escarole, whose sharp taste it shares. It's a strikingly attractive plant that comes in varieties ranging from green and bronze through maroon, red, and pink. It is also nutritious, supplying vitamins C, E, and K in addition to iron, magnesium, and zinc.

PICK YOUR POT

Grows well in a self-watering container. Plant six to eight seedlings in a large container.

GROW IT

For a spring crop, direct-seed when soil temperatures reach 45°F (7°C) or start seeds indoors eight weeks before the last frost date. Transplant to containers around the last frost date. For fall crops, direct-seed starting in late summer. Sow two or three seeds ¼ inch deep and eight inches apart and thin with scissors to one plant from each cluster. Radicchio turns bitter and may bolt in warm weather. Because of this, it is usually better grown as a fall and winter crop than as a summer crop.

BUG OFF

Flea beetles often plague radicchio. Growing plants under lightweight row covers is the best way to prevent infestation.

EAT IT

Harvest radicchio as soon as the heads form in the center and are firm; don't bother with the outer leaves. Radicchio is very hardy and can be harvested far into winter, especially if it is protected with a row cover.

PICK YOUR PLANT

'**Chioggia Red Preco**': round, purple red, with white veining

'**Fiero**': think Romaine lettuce but in burgundy with white ribs

'**Indigo**': burgundy-red with white midribs and a rounded shape; bolt resistant and fast growing

'**Palla di Fuoco Rossa**': "Balls of red fire!" — and indeed they are; round, deep burgundy with white veins; bolt resistant

This young radicchio is temporarily sharing space with some spinach; by the time the radicchio begins to mature, the spinach will have been harvested.

RADISHES

(*Raphanus sativus*)

Radishes are often the first vegetable gardeners grow, because they germinate easily and mature quickly. They do, however, need a constant supply of water and nutrients or they'll become tough and pithy. Radishes can get what they need in a self-watering container filled with compost-based soil.

Harvest these 'Cherry Bell' radishes when they're about the size of a large marble.

PICK YOUR POT

Radishes are happy in a self-watering container with at least six inches of soil depth.

GROW IT

Direct-sow radish seeds ½ inch deep, any time from early spring onward. Radishes can go into containers with seedling plants of other kinds or into containers that later in the gardening year will be home for transplants. Radishes grow quickly; they'll proceed from seedling to harvest in three or four weeks. If you want to harvest all season, do succession plantings every week or so.

BUG OFF

Radishes are a favored food of flea beetles, but the damage is usually only aesthetic. If the flea beetles in your garden are numerous enough to stunt the radishes' growth, plant the radishes all together and protect them with a row cover.

EAT IT

Radishes are at their prime for a very short time; the whole crop will mature over three or four days. Harvest them when they're the size of a large marble. Radishes left in the ground to grow bigger will turn pithy and bitter, and will split. Harvest radishes as soon as they're ready and store them in the refrigerator, where they'll stay in good condition for two or three weeks.

PICK YOUR PLANT

'**Cherry Bell**': a classic radish, round, bright red outside and snowy white inside

'**Easter Egg**': actually a radish mix, with reds, purples, and whites maturing over an extended period

'**D'Avignon**': traditional French variety, three to four inches long, cylindrical; red with white tips; matures in three weeks

SPINACH

(*Spinacia oleracea*)

*S*pinach is a natural for container growing. It tastes best if it grows quickly and evenly so that the plants are still tender at maturity, and that's best accomplished with a self-watering container. Although it does not like heat, it's the most frost-resistant plant I've ever grown, and actually tastes better after a frost. It regularly survives temperatures of –25°F (–32°C) in our unheated greenhouse and begins producing salads by late March.

PICK YOUR POT

If you want to grow spinach plants to maturity, plant four to six in a large self-watering container. If you plan to harvest baby spinach, space plants about three inches apart.

GROW IT

Direct-sow in early spring as soon as the soil temperature reaches 50°F (10°C). For baby greens, space plants about one inch apart and harvest when the leaves are three to four inches long. If you plan to grow the plants to maturity, plant seeds an inch apart and thin to three inches apart. The rest is easy; just make sure there's water in the reservoir. For a fall/winter crop, start planting again in late July. Given some protection, a spinach container garden will go on producing greens far into December.

These 'Space' spinach plants will be harvested long before their sweet potato container-mates need the soil space.

EAT IT

Pick individual leaves or wait and harvest the whole plant. The harvest is over when the plant begins to elongate and form a central stem that will become the flower stalk. At that point, pick the leaves and pull the plants.

PICK YOUR PLANT

'Space': high-yielding with an upright growth habit and relatively slow to bolt

'Olympia': an excellent fall crop because it is very resistant to freezing. Not recommended as a spring crop, because it bolts in hot weather.

CULINARY COUSIN

When is a spinach not a spinach? When it's New Zealand spinach, more properly known as tetragonia (*Tetragonia tetragonioides*). Tetragonia tastes like spinach, but is a larger, spreading plant. It provides a continual harvest of young leaf tips all summer, long after even the most bolt-resistant spinaches have gone to flower. The downside of tetragonia is that (unlike spinach) it is frost sensitive. Hence, at the end of the season, when the spinach I planted in late summer is thriving, tetragonia gives up the ghost.

STRAWBERRIES

(*Fragaria* spp.)

If there's a dessert that tops strawberry shortcake made with fresh, homegrown strawberries, I haven't yet encountered it. You can have a pale imitation of it with berries picked who-knows-how-long-ago and purchased at the grocery store, but the only way to have the real thing is to grow your own. And you can do it in a container. Strawberries are very easy to grow. All they need is fertile soil and a steady supply of water.

This self-watering strawberry planter will provide a home for a dozen plants.

PICK YOUR POT

I grow strawberries in a self-watering version of a strawberry planter; it has room for eight plants in small pockets bulging out from the sides and another four plants in the larger top opening. Any container with a soil depth of about eight inches would work, but this container has the advantage of growing a dozen plants in a container with a fairly small footprint.

GROW IT

Strawberry plants should be planted so that the crown (the place where the leaf stems emerge) is just even with the soil surface. If planted too deep, strawberries will rot. Getting the plants into the pockets of this container takes a bit of doing. Start by filling the pot to the level of the first pockets with moist container soil. Hold a plant with one hand from the outside of the container and make a hole with the other hand inside the container. The roots should be able to drop straight down, not be bunched up right below the crown. Push soil from the center of the pot into the pocket; once the plant is stabilized, add soil in a small amount through the pocket hole until the crown is level with the soil. Add more soil to the second level of pockets and repeat. Then add still more soil until you can plant in the large top opening.

Although container-grown strawberry plants can bear fruit the first year, I'd like the plants to spend the first year concentrating their energy on root growth so they'll be able to produce a better harvest the second year. Toward this end, I clip blossoms and runners from the first-year plants and get my first crop the second year.

Bug Off

Slugs will eat strawberries if given the opportunity. Keep the planter up off the ground so it's harder for slugs to attack. See chapter nine for other slug-battling suggestions.

Eat It

Strawberries are perfectly ripe for a very short time. A perfectly ripe berry is all red, without any white at the tip, but it is a very special red, almost glistening. As soon as the red darkens a bit and picks up just a hint of dullness (matte instead of glossy) the berry is too ripe and has started to lose sweetness and that subtle firmness that just barely resists the tooth. It's a bit of extra work, but I like to clip the berries from the plant with scissors so I don't bruise the fruit.

Pick Your Plant

Alpine strawberries: a miniature strawberry plant producing small fruits about twice the size of wild strawberries; plants are compact and produce very few runners

'Sarian': produces a small-to-medium-size berry over a long season and is advertised to produce a crop the first year

'Tristar': generally recommended for containers, and the one I grow; bears over a long season, from June to October

If this 'Tristar' strawberry isn't perfectly ripe, it's certainly within a few hours of getting there.

A SPRING TRIM

The strawberry planter at left wintered over in an unheated greenhouse, where temperatures went as low as −20°F (−29°C). We trimmed off the dead runners to give the new plantlets room to grow, and to reduce the risk of fungal infection.

SUMMER SQUASH

(*Cucurbita pepo*)

U nlike winter squash, which vines and twines anywhere and everywhere it wants to, summer squash is a tamer, more cooperative beast. It does take some room, and it'll do best in a large container, but summer squash is a bush rather than a vine, and generally (though not always) stays within the boundaries of its home container.

'Eight Ball' zucchini tastes like a regular zucchini, but it sure doesn't look like one.

PICK YOUR POT

The secret with summer squashes is to start with a fairly large self-watering container. These are sizable plants with a lot of foliage; they need a lot of nourishment, and a lot of soil to provide that nourishment. They also need a lot of water; a mature squash plant will go through as much water as a mature tomato plant, a gallon or more a day. If the reservoir of your container doesn't hold at least that much, you'll be adding water more than once a day.

GROW IT

Summer squash varieties are all "short season"; they have plenty of time to produce a crop in even the northern part of the country, so they can be direct sown in a container once the soil temperature is dependably above 70°F (21°C). These are heat-loving plants and are designed so they won't germinate until they are guaranteed nice summer weather to grow in. Summer squash seeds will just sit there and rot in cold, damp soil. Plant three seeds about ¾ inch deep in a large round or square container. Thin to the best plant when the first true leaf emerges. Row covers will speed growth and protect against temperature fluctuations; to allow pollination, remove the covers when blossoms appear.

If you just can't wait for that first savory meal of lightly sautéed baby squash, you can start your plants indoors and transplant them outdoors when the weather is right. But don't try to get too much of a head start. Squash plants are fussy and don't like to have their roots disturbed; the bigger the plant at the time of transplanting, the harder it is to avoid disturbing the roots, so two or three weeks before transplanting is about right. Start three or four seeds in a four-inch pot. When the plants are up and growing well, thin all but the best one with scissors. Transplant carefully after the danger of frost is past, hardening off the plants for about a week before transplanting. Summer squash are, in my experience, pretty trouble-free. They're big plants, though, and may need a dose of liquid fertilizer when they start producing fruits.

BUG OFF

In theory, summer squash should be plagued by the same pests that trouble winter squash and cucumbers — cucumber beetles, squash bugs, and vine borers. In practice, I've had pest-infested winter squash growing in the same garden as pest-free summer squash of various varieties. A lightweight row cover will protect summer squash against pests and provide some heat for faster growth. Be sure to remove it when blossoms appear.

EAT IT

This is where you reap — or fail to reap — the rewards of growing summer squash in your own garden. If you wait to harvest your summer squash until it looks like what you see for sale at the supermarket, you've missed the boat. Summer squash is at its best when young and tender and considerably smaller than what you'll see in the market. Harvest yellow squash and zucchini when the fruits are no more than four to five inches long and the skin is still tender. Pattypan and scallop squash lose flavor when they grow beyond four inches in diameter, and taste best at only two to three inches. As long as you keep harvesting the squash at this early stage, the plant will keep producing more.

PICK YOUR PLANT

'Eight Ball': small, dark green zucchinis that are . . . round; mature when they're a little bigger than a pool ball

'Seneca Prolific': yellow straightneck with an early yield

'Sunburst': a pattypan variety with many "flying saucer" fruits on a compact plant

'Zephyr': a yellow straightneck that is actually two-toned, with a light green bottom to complement its yellow top

This 'Seneca Prolific' yellow squash is actually a bit past prime eating stage, but it will still taste garden fresh.

SQUASH CROP COMBO

Summer squashes won't move into their container until frost danger is past, and they won't be needing all the space in the container for a while after that — time enough to get four lettuces or spinach plants going in the corners of the container about a month before the frost date. The lettuces will be ready to harvest by the time the squash takes over the container. Radishes planted in the squash container in early spring will be long gone before the squash plants take over.

SWEET POTATOES

(*Ipomoea batatas*)

I love to find foods that are both tasty and good for me. Sweet potatoes are just such a food. They're generally grown much farther south than where I live and garden, but there are some sweet potato varieties that will produce a crop even here in the cold North. Fortunately, those varieties grow very well in self-watering containers.

The foliage from two sweet potato plants, a 'Vardaman' and a 'Georgia Jet', fills this large self-watering container.

With flowers like these, sweet potatoes would be tempting to grow even if they didn't provide me with food.

PICK YOUR POT

Choose a medium self-watering container for a single plant; two will grow in a large container.

GROW IT

Sweet potato plants grow from *slips*, the sprouts that form sweet potatoes. They are sometimes available at garden centers and in seed catalogs. Slips are generally sold in bundles of a dozen or so; if that's more than you want to grow, get together with neighbors and share.

Plant slips outdoors only after all danger of frost is past. (In practice, that may be as much as two weeks after the last frost date.) You can stretch the growing season a bit if you're willing and able to move sweet potato containers inside when frost threatens. Or use row covers; the plants will enjoy the extra warmth. Grow sweet potatoes in a sunny place, especially if you live north of their natural range.

In the sort of container mix I use, sweet potatoes do not need extra fertilizer; they actually respond poorly to a surplus of nitrogen, producing lots of foliage and few sweet potatoes.

EAT IT

Harvesting container-grown sweet potatoes is simple. Cut the plants at soil level, dump the container onto a tarp or some newspaper, and paw through the soil and glean the tubers.

PICK YOUR PLANT

'Beauregard': relatively short season and good for baking

'Georgia Jet': can produce edible roots in 75 days

'Vardaman': a compact plant well suited to container growing

Swiss Chard

(*Beta vulgaris,* Cicla Group)

Swiss chard reminds me of a multipurpose tool. It does many things — it makes a good salad ingredient, it's tasty steamed, and it has the virtue of starting production early in the season and continuing right on through the summer and into the frosty days of late fall. It is also, at least in some of its varieties, stunningly beautiful.

PICK YOUR POT

Container choice depends on how many plants you want to grow and whether you're harvesting salad-size greens or mature leaves. Even a window box will grow Swiss chard.

GROW IT

Direct-sow beginning in early spring and continue into midsummer. Spacing depends on how you want to harvest: for salad greens, about one inch apart; for cooking, four to five inches apart; for continuous harvest of the outer leaves, about eight inches apart.

BUG OFF

Nothing seems to bother Swiss chard, except for the occasional slug. See chapter nine for slug-control strategies.

EAT IT

For salad greens, harvest by clipping the plants ½ inch above the soil at about five weeks. A new set of leaves will grow, but they may not be quite as tasty as the first set. For cooking, harvest the whole plant at soil level. For continuous harvest, snip off the outer stalks with a sharp knife.

PICK YOUR PLANT

'**Bright Lights**': a garden rainbow; the stems may be gold, pink, orange, purple, red, yellow, or white, all with leaves of dark green or bronze

'**Bright Yellow**': yellow stems, green leaves; mild taste

'**Fordhook Giant**': the old-time, standard Swiss chard

'**Ruby Red**': bright red stems and green leaves; not as frost tolerant as other chards; delay planting until after the last frost date

These are just two of the many color variations that spring from a packet of 'Bright Lights' chard seeds.

TOMATOES

(*Lycopersicon lycopersicum*)

If you could grow just one vegetable in your container garden, what would it be? For the overwhelming majority of gardeners, the answer is "tomatoes." Tomatoes are America's favorite vegetable, period. Fortunately, tomatoes grow very, very well in self-watering containers.

'Sweet 100' cherry tomatoes in all stages of ripeness appear on the plant simultaneously. As the first frost nears, clip off the clusters of small, green tomatoes that will not have time to ripen on the vine.

PICK YOUR POT

A full-size tomato plant needs a container with a soil capacity of at least 20 quarts and a water capacity of at least a gallon, but I like to use an even bigger container (40 quarts of soil and at least a two-gallon reservoir). A bigger water reservoir means you won't have to water every day. A 40-quart container with a four-gallon reservoir will support two tomato plants or one compact tomato and a few companions like a pepper or eggplant, some lettuce, a basil plant or two. (In any combination, the fast-growing tomato will fare better than whatever grows with it. You'll get a more productive pepper plant if you grow it alone or with less demanding plants than tomatoes.)

GROW IT

Tomatoes originate in a much warmer climate than they will enjoy where they are asked to grow in most of the country. They like warmth. They like sunlight. Tomatoes are, with a few exceptions, big plants; all that biomass needs to be created by photosynthesis, and you can't have photosynthesis without the *photo* part. So be sure to give tomatoes the best seats in the house — wherever they will get the longest time in the sun. Tomatoes are also water hogs. A mature tomato plant will use a gallon of water every day. So, all else being equal, put your tomato plants within easy reach of your water supply.

Starting tomato plants isn't difficult, but it requires some equipment and some sunny space (or, better yet, a fluorescent light). If you have the desire and the space and the equipment, starting your own can be rewarding and give you a jump on the gardening season. You'll already be growing something while almost everybody else is just dreaming.

If you start your own plants, you'll get to try varieties you aren't likely to find at local garden centers. A well-stocked garden center or nursery may have a half-dozen varieties. A typical seed catalog will have three dozen or more.

That said, we usually buy seedlings for most of the tomatoes we raise in containers. That's true even though we start seeds for almost all the tomatoes we grow in the earth garden. Why? In the earth garden, most of the tomatoes are destined for sauce or juice instead of fresh eating. We need a large number of plants divided among just a few varieties, usually proven performers rather than "maybe it will work" novelties. We'll use most of the seeds in three or four packets.

It's a different story with the container tomatoes. Virtually all the container tomatoes end up in salads, sandwiches, or fresh salsa. Containers somehow stimulate the adventurer in me. Why not try something I've never tried before? Or try a tomato just because I like the name or because it's an odd color or it has a wonderful story attached to it? But I'm not going to try a dozen each of such novelties; one or maybe two will be enough. So whereas in the earth garden I want many examples of a few varieties, in the container garden I want just a few examples (often just one) of many varieties. If the variety I want is available at a nursery, I can likely buy a well-started plant for no more than the cost of a packet of seeds, most of which I'm not going to use.

BUYING TIPS

So, I've decided to buy my tomato plants rather than start them myself. It's Memorial Day, and therefore time to plant tomatoes in the garden. Off to the garden center! And I'll choose the biggest, tallest plants I can find, preferably with some blossoms so I can get a head start with my crop. Well, no. Big time, no. If I do it that way, I've managed to do just about everything wrong, and my tomato year is off to a very poor start.

Let's start over. First of all, I'll make my tomato-buying trip earlier in the year, as soon as tomato seedlings first appear for sale. The hardest part is over once a seedling has emerged from the soil and grown a few sets of true leaves. From there on, the plants are likely to get better care from me than in a greenhouse, where they will have to compete for attention (and light and water) with hundreds or thousands of other plants. The first thing I can give them is a new and bigger home. A tomato plant's root system is the key to its success in life; a tomato ready for transplanting should be growing in at least a four-inch pot. Very few nursery tomato plants get to live in four-inch pots; because

If the tomato plants you buy at a garden center have blossoms, clip them off. Seedlings need to grow roots before they have the strength to set fruit.

DETERMINING WHAT'S INDETERMINATE

Seed catalogs generally identify tomatoes as either determinate or indeterminate. *Determinate* tomatoes grow as bushes rather than vines. They reach a certain size, and then don't get much bigger. They set fruit, mature and ripen it, and then go into decline; their work is done. *Indeterminate* tomatoes are a different sort of beast. They're vines, and they go right on growing for as long as the weather allows, setting more fruit along the way. Indeterminate tomatoes, in favorable growing conditions, can be taller than the gardener growing them.

of that, they become pot-bound and stressed. (The blossoms on some small, skinny nursery tomatoes are actually a sign of stress; the plant can't grow more roots, so it responds by hurrying into the next phase of life long before it has the strength to bear fruit. If you find blossoms on tomato plants before or soon after transplanting, clip them off. The plant needs to grow more roots and foliage before taking on the work of growing and ripening fruit.)

Whether I buy my plants early or late, I want short, stocky ones, not tall, lanky ones. Check any plants you buy at a nursery or garden center for signs of insect damage or disease. Leaves should be dark green without holes, missing pieces, brown or black spots, or curled edges.

A 'Jet Star' tomato gets all the support it needs from a tomato cage. The cage, in turn, is supported by its lowest crossbars resting on the soil surface.

STARTING TIPS

Start tomatoes indoors no more than five to six weeks before the last frost date. You can start seeds in a flat or, the way I do it, in two-inch cells. I start seeds in the same peat/compost mix that I use in containers, and I have not had problems with damping-off (a fungal disease that sometimes affects seedlings). Not everybody thinks the way I do, though, and most authorities would recommend a sterile, peat-based starting mix. Either way, keep the soil moist but not soggy, and the temperature between 75 and 90°F (24–32°C). (Tomatoes will germinate at slightly lower temperatures, but it takes longer.) If you're using a fertilizer-free starting mix, fertilize the seedlings with liquid seaweed fertilizer.

About 10 days after germination, when the first true leaves have appeared, transplant into four-inch pots. Set the plants deeper than they were in the starting flat, so only the top leaves show above the soil. Water regularly but lightly; the soil should never be either dry or soggy, just moist all the time.

Harden off seedlings for about two weeks before you expect to plant them outdoors. At first, move them to a shady spot for an hour or so, then back inside. Increase the outdoor time about an hour a day; it can be longer on cloudy days. By the time they are ready for life in the garden, the plants should be used to being out all day and able to stand full sun for most of the day.

When soil temperatures are at least 55°F (13°C) and night-time air temperatures don't go below 40, it's time to transplant. Plan to transplant in the cool of the day, and shade the plants from full sun for a few days, with overturned pots or the like. Plant tomatoes in containers deeper than they grew in pots, trimming off any leaves that will be buried. (Tomatoes have the ability to grow roots from buried stems; each time you transplant them deeper, they grow more roots.) In a relatively shallow container (eight inches), lay the plant down, so most of the stem will be buried, and make a pillow of soil to curve the top of the plant gently upward. The plant will get the hint and take off straight up in a day or so. If you're using a container mix plus fertilizer, fertilize again in about six weeks.

TRELLISING

Except for very compact plants like 'Micro Tom', 'Tiny Tim', and 'Window Box Roma', tomato plants grown in containers need outside support of some kind. But tomatoes, if they were in charge of how they were to grow, would not climb trellises or want to be tied to stakes; they'd crawl along the ground like the vines they are. And tomatoes would not, on their own, limit themselves to one main stem; they'd send out side shoots all over the place, each of which would become a major stem. It's gardeners who want tomatoes to behave themselves and grow in a stately, upright manner, easy to tend and harvest.

Tomatoes — the ones called indeterminate, at least (see "Determining What's Indeterminate," page 201) — have another preferred growth habit that operates at cross-purposes to my intentions. Tomatoes don't seem to notice that fall is coming, and with it growth-ending frost. They'll go right on growing and growing and making new flowers, setting new fruits that have no chance of ripening before the season ends. Pruning is the way gardeners tame tomatoes and get them to behave as we think they ought.

If grown in a cage trellis, tomatoes can be left to their own devices until later in the season. About a month before frost is expected, prune the growing tips of all the stems and remove blossoms and small fruits that will not have time to mature and ripen. This way, the plant puts its energy into maturing fruits that have already set.

Growing tomatoes on a single trellis, on a stake, or on a cord suspended from a crossbar requires a more drastic style of pruning. Each and every sucker that appears on the main stem must be pruned off. Otherwise, each sucker becomes a new stem and the tomato plant very quickly becomes impossible to trellis. When the plant grows to the top of the trellis, stop its growth by pruning the terminal shoot. The benefit to this method is that the plant does not become top-heavy and overwhelm its trellis.

These 'Sweet Baby Girl' cherry tomatoes are growing on a trellis attached to the container.

BUG OFF

Many of the diseases that may trouble tomatoes are soilborne and therefore not likely to affect container-grown plants. The only pest of note is the tomato hornworm (see chapter nine). Watch for it as you contemplate your tomato plants, and if you find one, pick it off and drop it in a can of soapy water.

Suckers grow between the plant's main stem and its side branches. Each sucker will become a new major stem unless you clip it off.

EAT IT

To avoid damaging the plant, clip ripe tomatoes from the vine with scissors. Tomatoes can ripen after they are picked; before the first hard frost, pick all the fruits that have begun to ripen and bring them inside. Most of them will ripen on a windowsill in a few days. (If a container is portable enough, bring the whole plant indoors and let the tomatoes ripen on the vine.)

PICK YOUR PLANT

There are so many tomato varieties out there that I hesitate to recommend any. What works for me and tickles my taste buds might not work for you. So take my suggestions as you would a ripe tomato — with a grain of salt. Ask your gardening neighbors, and visit local greenhouses. That's how we found most of the tomatoes we grow.

'Jet Star': an old favorite here in Vermont; full-size, seven- to eight-ounce fruits; a compact growth habit; relatively short growing season

'Micro Tom': more of a novelty than a food source; the plant is only about six inches tall, and the few fruits are the size of marble; it's cute, and will live in even a small hanging planter

'Rose': an heirloom variety, reputed to be Amish in origin; excellent flavor

'Siletz': an early full-size slicing tomato on a compact plant

'Sun Gold': sweet, prolific cherry with a deep golden color

'Sweet Baby Girl': a red cherry with a compact growth habit

'Sweet 100': a prolific red cherry tomato

'Tiny Tim': a very compact cherry that doesn't need a trellis

'Window Box Roma': compact plant bearing full-size paste tomatoes; does not need a trellis

TURNIPS

(*Brassica rapa*)

The turnips we're talking about here are not the big ones stored away for winter eating, the ones colonists used to feed to their cattle. (As a turnip-dreading lad, I always thought that was a very good use for this humble root.) The turnips we'll grow in a container are small, sweet, and tender with tasty and nutritious greens. They don't store well and aren't meant to; these turnips are a summer food, steamed, sautéed, or added to a soup, and the greens are good cooked or raw.

PICK YOUR POT

Choose a deep self-watering container; turnips have a long tap-root and need at least eight inches of soil depth.

GROW IT

Direct-sow turnips any time from early spring onward, ¼–½ inch deep and one inch apart. When the tops have developed to a useful size, pull every other turnip and let the rest grow to harvest size of one to two inches. In a compost-based soil, no further fertilizing should be required. Small succession plantings a week or 10 days apart will keep you supplied all summer.

BUG OFF

Turnips are host to flea beetles and root maggots, the parents of which lay eggs in the soil. Neither pest can bother turnips grown under a row cover.

EAT IT

Summer turnips taste best when harvested at "radish" size, about an inch or two in diameter. At that stage the greens are still in nice shape too. Harvest turnips when they're at the prime size; they'll keep better in the refrigerator than they will in the soil.

PICK YOUR PLANT

'**Hakurei**': white, with a flattened round shape and so sweet it can be eaten raw

'**Purple Top White Globe**': smooth, round roots are white below the soil and purple above

'Purple Top White Globe' turnips look an awful lot like radishes, and should be harvested at the same size.

WINTER SQUASH

(*Cucurbita* spp.)

I like the challenge of growing something you'd never think to grow in a container, and I'm always on the lookout for good-looking plants with pretty flowers — both areas where winter squash scores some points. Most winter squash plants are way too big for a container garden, and their chosen growth habit is to roam all over the neighborhood. There are, however, a few varieties with small fruits and more compact vines that are suited to life in a container. (They are described in catalogs as "short-vined" or "semi-bush.")

Even a compact squash like this 'Ponca Baby Butternut' can develop a yearning to travel outside its container.

PICK YOUR POT

Winter squashes respond well to the continual moisture they get in a self-watering container. One plant per large container will be plenty.

GROW IT

Winter squash plants take a long time to nurture and ripen their fruits; even the small-fruited varieties listed below need three frost-free months. Unless you have a growing season at least that long, plan to start winter squash indoors or purchase plants at a nursery. Winter squash, like their summer cousins, do not like to be transplanted; the bigger the plant, the more susceptible it is to transplanting stress. Therefore, start plants about three weeks before the last frost date and grow them right from the get-go in a four-inch pot, where they'll stay until transplanted to a container. Sow three seeds about ¾ inch deep and try to maintain a temperature of about 70°F (21°C).

Thin to the strongest plant by clipping the others with scissors. Harden off the plants for about a week before transplanting. When the danger of frost is past and the soil temperature is about 70°F (21°C) transplant the seedlings into a large self-watering container, being careful not to disturb their roots.

Eat It

Winter squash harvested too soon is a total waste. It won't keep well — and, much more important, it won't taste good. The flesh will be watery and bland. The key to great winter squash is timely harvest. When a winter squash is ripe, the stem begins to shrivel and dry and the skin hardens to the point where you can't gouge it with a thumbnail. Butternut squash will be evenly tan in color without any green stripes at the stem end.

Squash plants are sensitive to frost, but they can tolerate a few degrees below freezing if protected by a row cover. (Toss a blanket on top of the cover to be on the safe side.)

Handle harvested fruits gently, and don't carry them by the stems, which may break off, drastically shortening the storage life of the fruit. Cure winter squash for five to seven sunny days outside, but cover them or move them inside if frost threatens.

Pick Your Plant

'Burpee's Butterbush': a butternut with a compact growth habit and short vines six feet long at most

'Bush Delicata': short season; compact bush growth habit with a three-foot spread

'Bush Table Queen': three-foot-wide plant that produces four-inch acorn squashes in 80 days

'Heart of Gold': compact plant that produces five-inch fruits with sweet, tender orange flesh

'Ponca Baby Butternut': relatively short season butternut, producing two-pound fruits

TILTING THE ODDS YOUR WAY

In the best of years, winter squashes sometimes fail to ripen in the cooler parts of the country. To increase the chances you'll get a good harvest, try some or all of these "season stretchers."

- Grow winter squash in a dark-colored container to warm the soil.
- A few days before transplanting, cover the container with black or IRT plastic to warm the soil.
- Grow beneath a row cover, removing it when blossoms appear. The cover will provide a warmer environment and protect against late frosts.

'Heart of Gold' is a compact sweet dumpling squash that bears five-inch fruits.

CHAPTER THIRTEEN

HERBS FOR EVERY POT

Many people start container gardening with herbs, and for good reason. For the most part, herbs need little care and adapt readily to life in a pot. A lot of the herbs I've tried grow very well in self-watering containers, though some prefer a drier, traditional pot; they actually taste better with a little stress. Here are the plants I've found to do best in each situation.

BASIL

(Ocimum basilicum)

For most people, basil is an herb; for me it's a vegetable. When our family uses basil, it's not as a garnish or a spice; it's a big part of the meal, whether it's as the main ingredient of a pesto or as the "lettuce" part of a BLT. Basil is definitely one of those herbs that need a little stress in their life; if you grow it in rich soil and water it well, you'll have a big, beautiful plant that doesn't have anywhere near the flavor of basil grown in marginally fertile soil and watered sparingly.

Four varieties of basil cohabit well in this self-watering container. Clockwise from top left: 'Osmin Purple', 'Genovese', 'Sweet Thai', and 'Lime'.

PICK YOUR POT

If you most want a pretty plant — and some of the purple basils tempt us in that direction — then grow basil in a self-watering container in the same planting mix you'd use for vegetables and keep the reservoir full. Basil is not very demanding and gets along with most other plants. (Grown with a big bully of a plant like a full-size tomato, though, basil will get the short end of the stick and languish a bit. It will grow and produce a crop of leaves, but it won't get nearly as big as it would in its own pot.)

If you want basil with full flavor, grow it in a traditional container and let the soil dry some between waterings. Don't let the plant wilt, but don't keep the soil constantly moist.

GROW IT

Most basils — and there are many of them — are native to the Mediterranean. They like sunlight and they like heat. When it comes to cold weather, basils are the wimps of the garden; they aren't just frost sensitive, like tomatoes or peppers; they're *cold* sensitive. Nighttime temperatures below 50°F (10°C) will stress a basil plant, and it will have trouble recovering.

Keeping this in mind, don't put basil plants outdoors until nighttime temperatures will be continually above 50°F (10°C). As a container grower, you can stretch the rules a bit if you're willing to move your basil containers inside on cool nights. You'll pick up extra growth from any abundant sunshine during the day. We compromise by stalling our major basil plantings until warm weather and planting a few small and easily portable containers that we can move indoors when chilly weather threatens. That way we have enough early basil for salads and pesto and a larger crop later for freezing and drying.

At the other end of the season, plan on harvesting all the basil before the first frost. We bring indoors a couple of basil plants in small containers before the frost, to keep us in fresh basil into the winter.

We usually buy transplants or start basil plants from seed inside. Basil seeds are small, so they should be just barely covered with finely sifted soil and kept moist. Germination is spotty — expect around 60 percent — so plant more seeds than you think you'll need and then clip any extra seedlings. Alternatively, you can plant basil directly in containers once temperatures are dependably warm. Plant the seeds two to three inches apart and thin to four to eight inches, depending on the expected size of the mature plants.

Eat It

You can harvest leaves as soon as the plants are big enough not to miss the foliage. The best flavor, though, is in the smaller leaves making up the growing tips of a plant. Concentrating your harvest there has the added benefit of stimulating yet more tips and inducing the plant to become fuller and bushier. Basil flowers are also edible, both as buds and as blooms, but the leaves taste better before the plant flowers.

Harvested basil will stay fresh for a few days in a glass of water, but don't refrigerate it; basil doesn't like cool temperatures even after it is harvested. Dried basil is worth the trouble too. The flavor is likely to be better than that of basil bought in a supermarket, and you can dry varieties you'll never find on any market's spice shelf. Basil can also be frozen, as pesto, as a puree, or as leaves just packed into a plastic bag. It can also be preserved in vinegar.

Bug Off

As long as its temperature preferences are respected, basil is not bothered by any pests or diseases.

The flowers of spicy bush basil are gorgeous, but they signal the start of a bitter harvest for foliage.

Pick Your Plant

There are lots of basils. Pesto basils. Scented basils, spicy, lime, lemon, cinnamon, licorice basils! Even sacred, or holy, basil. Many catalogs list more than a dozen varieties. In theory, at least, all basil varieties can be grown in containers — even the largest basil plants are considerably smaller than, for instance, a tomato plant. Some varieties, though, because of their compact size, make a particularly good choice for containers. And some are very pretty and make a nice addition to a garden that feeds the spirit as well as the body. (We grow a lot more purple basil than we eat, just because purple is a nice color to have in the garden palette.)

'Genovese': an Italian basil with some resistance to bolting

'Osmin Purple': dark purple leaves with pale lilac flowers on a 16- to 20-inch plant

Spicy bush basil: an eight-inch plant with small, attractive leaves and a spicy taste

'Summerlong': about a foot high, bushy, and much less likely to bolt; a good variety to bring inside before frost for a winter crop of fresh basil

BORAGE

(*Borago officinalis*)

Is it an herb? Or is it an edible flower? Perhaps it doesn't really make any difference. In garden books and seed catalogs, I find borage most often among the herbs. That said, you'll want to grow it for its amazing blue flowers even if you've no use for the leaves. The leaves and flowers have a mild, cucumber-like flavor and are especially good in salads.

The fuzzy flower buds of borage taste like cucumber, and the flowers attract bees to our garden.

PICK YOUR POT

Borage has the potential to be a large plant, especially when it gets all the water and food it likes. In a self-watering container, it will become a two- to three-foot plant and probably should grow alone, because it will crowd out other plants. If you grow borage this way, choose a medium container with at least eight inches of soil depth. Grown in a traditional container and therefore not able to get unlimited access to water, borage will behave in a more restrained manner.

GROW IT

You can start borage indoors in early spring or direct-seed it outdoors after the last frost date, but since you'll really need only one borage plant to supply all the leaves and flowers you can eat, you're better off buying it at the local nursery. Don't let the plant get too large before transplanting, and transplant it carefully; it has a long taproot. Don't fertilize borage, and don't worry if you miss a few waterings. Pick flowers and leaves to keep the plant producing.

EAT IT

The leaves can be eaten raw in salads or steamed like spinach; the young foilage is more tender and has a milder flavor. The flowers are a colorful garnish in salads and can also be made into a tea.

BUG OFF

Pests and diseases do not appear to be a problem.

PICK YOUR PLANT

Most borage plants have blue flowers, but there is also a variety with white blooms. Sometimes there are pink flowers among the blue ones as well.

CHAMOMILE

(*Matricaria recutita*)

The flowers of chamomile (actually, the yellow center of the flowers, minus the white petals) make a soothing tea that carries an aroma suggestive of apples and pineapple. In addition to being delicious, it is easy to grow in containers and is also quite decorative. Why not plant a pot of tea on your patio?

PICK YOUR POT

German chamomile, the variety that makes the best tea, matures as an upright plant about a foot and a half tall. It will grow well in small to medium traditional or self-watering containers that are at least eight inches deep. Chamomile does need a steady supply of water; if you are unable to water regularly, a self-watering container is preferable.

GROW IT

German chamomile is an annual that can be grown from seed or transplants. Start seeds indoors a month or so before the last frost. The seeds are small and take at least a week and a half to germinate; they must stay moist the entire time. Transplant outdoors when the danger of frost is past. When the plants are young, they can't tolerate full sun; grow them in partial shade for the first few weeks.

EAT IT

Of all the many parts that make up a chamomile plant, only one — the center of the small, daisylike flower — is used. Pick the flowers when the petals have just begun to curl toward the center of the flower and dry them on a cookie sheet in a warm, well-ventilated place. Remove the petals either before or after drying, whichever way is easier for you and results in the least damage to the yellow centers.

PICK YOUR PLANT

'**Bona**': a smaller plant with very sweet blossoms

'**Lutea**': large blossoms, and many of them

Roman chamomile: a perennial (*Chamaemelum nobile*) also grown for tea, but tends to be more bitter

Chamomile makes a calming tea, in addition to being a cheerful container planting.

CHIVES

(*Allium schoenoprasum*)

I can't imagine a potato salad without chives, or a potato soup, either. And chive blossoms jazz up any salad that suffers from too much green. In the early spring, when not much is growing in the garden except the garlic we planted last fall, the chives are up and ready to add a bit of spice to our mealtime.

Purple chive blossoms are sure to spice up any salad.

CULINARY COUSIN

Although they look a lot like chives, garlic chives, also known as Chinese leeks, are actually from a different branch of the allium family tree — known as *Allium tuberosum*. The flat, grasslike leaves with a hint of garlic can be used as a garlic substitute in salads or added late in the cooking process to sautéed vegetables. (They get slimy if cooked more than a few moments.) The white flowers are also edible. Grow as you would chives, but harvest lightly until the plants are well established.

PICK YOUR POT

Chives will grow in any sort of container, but they have a pretty good appetite for water and are therefore easier to tend in a self-watering container.

GROW IT

This hardy perennial plant is easy to grow. In fact, it's *too* easy to grow: given half a chance, chives will take over whatever little plot of ground they're given. You can grow chives in among annual plants in a container, but I prefer to grow them alone in a small pot that is easy to carry into the house for the winter. You can start chives from seed, but it takes a year for the plants to reach harvestable size. For the price of a packet of seeds you can buy a started plant in the local greenhouse and be harvesting chives in a month or so.

EAT IT

Clip the leaves and flowers as needed with scissors. Bring a pot of chives indoors for the winter; keep it watered and in a sunny window, and you'll have a touch of spring in your salads all winter long.

BUG OFF

Pests and diseases do not appear to be a problem.

PICK YOUR PLANT

Fine leaf: the standard culinary chives for eating fresh

CILANTRO

(*Coriandrum sativum*)

Grow this plant for its leaves, and it's called cilantro. But grow it for the seeds, and it's called coriander. The leaves have a fresh (some say lemony) taste and are a bit tangy; they're used in Oriental and Mexican cooking and in salsas or as a garnish. The toasted seeds are often used in curry dishes.

PICK YOUR POT

By any name, this plant is not happy in a self-watering container; it will quickly rot away if given constant moisture. Grow cilantro in a small to medium traditional container that's at least eight inches deep to accommodate its long taproot.

GROW IT

Direct-seed cilantro about ½ inch deep after all danger of frost is past. Germination takes about two weeks. Cilantro can be started indoors and (very carefully) transplanted while still young, but you'll have better results if you start the plant in the container it will live in. If you buy plants at a nursery, pick small ones without any buds or flowers. Cilantro will respond to hot weather by moving into seed-producing mode, and the leaves will droop and fall off. Give it more water during hot spells, but be careful of overwatering.

EAT IT

The leaves can be picked at any point, but they taste best in the cool of late spring and early summer. Cilantro leaves are best used fresh. They don't preserve well, by either drying or freezing, but can be made into pesto and then frozen.

The seeds are ready when the seed heads have just turned brown; gather them before they begin to scatter. Seeds should be dried before use. Spread them on a baking sheet and put them in the oven at 200°F (93°C) until dry. Or put the heads in a paper bag in a warm place; the seeds will ripen and drop from the heads. Store in an airtight jar.

BUG OFF

Pests and diseases do not appear to be a problem.

PICK YOUR PLANT

'Santo': a slow-bolting variety grown primarily for its foliage

Plant cilantro in a traditional pot; it prefers a bit of drought.

CULINARY COUSIN

Culantro is spelled almost like *cilantro*, and it tastes very much like it, but the two plants have no botanical relationship whatsoever. Unlike cilantro, culantro (*Eryngium foetidum*) prefers a bit of shade. It is a small plant and grows slowly. It makes a very good container plant and can grow happily indoors in the winter.

DILL

(*Anthenum graveolens*)

*D*ill is a versatile edible that finds its way into our diets at different stages of its life cycle. The wispy leaves add zest to potatoes, green beans, and onions. You can't have dill pickles without dill flowers, and dill seed is a staple of any spice rack. In addition to being tasty and beautiful, this plant comes with a bonus feature; it attracts beneficial insects to your container garden.

Though grown mostly for its foliage, fernleaf dill also has lovely, delicious seed heads.

PICK YOUR POT

Dill is a traditionalist when it comes to containers; a self-watering container provides it with too much water, and the plant dies. Grow dill in a medium traditional container at least 8 inches in diameter and 12 inches deep.

GROW IT

Dill can be started indoors and transplanted, but it has a long taproot and is fussy about transplanting. It generally does better if direct-seeded where it's going to live. Plant seeds outdoors after the last frost date. If you want to get an early harvest, start dill indoors in the pot where it will grow; move it outdoors when the weather warms a bit. Dill likes warm soil and is sensitive to even light frosts. Let the soil dry out a bit between waterings.

EAT IT

Harvest the leaves as soon as the plant is big enough that it won't miss a few. Harvest green dill heads just before bloom. Harvest the heads for seed when some of the seeds turn brown. Put the heads upside down in a ventilated paper bag to let the rest of the seeds mature and dry. Store in an airtight jar.

BUG OFF

Pests and disease do not appear to be a problem. In fact, dill's tiny, pale yellow flowers attract beneficial insects like green lacewings, whose larvae eat aphids and other garden pests.

VARIETIES

Bouquet: best grown for seed heads

Fernleaf: generally known as the best dill for containers

FENNEL

(*Foeniculum vulgare*)

There are two fennels: both are edible and are good as container plants. Sweet fennel is grown for its delicate, feathery leaves, tasty as a garnish in coleslaw or as an ingredient in salad dressing. Its edible seeds and anise-scented stems are used in tomato sauces, meatballs, sausages, and festive breads. Florence fennel forms a large bulb aboveground; the bulb and the stalks growing from it are edible, as are the foliage and seeds.

PICK YOUR POT

Fennel is a substantial plant, about two feet high and a foot across, and has a big taproot. In its native environs, fennel has to endure periods of very little water; because of that, it won't grow well in a self-watering container. Put it all together, and that means a fairly large traditional pot, at least 12 inches deep.

GROW IT

Fennel is sensitive to frost and should be started indoors about four weeks before the last frost date. Because it has a taproot, fennel is difficult to transplant after the first month.

Grow fennel in full sun and water intermittently, allowing the soil to dry somewhat between waterings. It won't need fertilizer, but it prefers its soil a bit on the sweet side, so add a tablespoon of lime to your potting mix.

EAT IT

Harvest fennel leaves whenever you need them. The stalks are best after the flower buds have formed but before they open. The bulb of Florence fennel is ready for eating when it is firm and around four inches across. Fennel does not store well, and should be used within a day or so of harvest.

Sweet fennel (green) and bronze fennel grow together in this traditional container of glazed clay.

The mature foliage of bronze fennel takes on a purplish hue.

BUG OFF

I haven't encountered any diseases that affect fennel, but there is one pest: the so-called parsley worm, the larval stage of the black swallowtail butterfly. It's difficult for me to call this a pest. I would rather say that fennel has one more virtue: it attracts and plays host to a beautiful butterfly. The "worm" is also not likely to damage the fennel plant, nor will it eat so much of the foliage that I won't have enough for myself.

PICK YOUR PLANT

Bronze fennel: decorative bronze-red foliage

Florence fennel: forms an edible bulb; if you harvest it for the bulb, you'll miss out on the seeds

Leaf fennel: particularly tasty foliage

Sweet fennel: does not form a bulb; foliage and stems are generally considered to be better tasting than those of Florence fennel

SAVING SEED FOR TEA

Harvesting fennel seeds is an easy way to stock up on herbal tea for the winter. Just as they begin to turn from their natural green to brown, clip the seed heads and put them in a paper bag to dry. The seeds will shake loose after a couple of weeks, after which they should be stored in an airtight container. It's actually a good idea to harvest the seeds whether or not you intend to use them, as fennel has been known to seed itself around. Unless you want lots of little fennel plants next spring, be sure to clip off those heads.

Although it can be used in any number of dishes, ground fennel seed makes a delicious, licoricy tea. Fennel tea is widely touted as a way to stimulate digestion and neutralize stomach acid, and was often prescribed by early Greek physicians. To make a serving of tea, steep one tablespoon of ground fennel seed in one cup of boiling water.

HYSSOP

(*Hyssopus officinalis*)

Like many other plants that fall into the "herb" category, hyssop has both edible flowers and edible leaves. The indigo flowers also attract beneficial insects — especially bees and butterflies — that help with pollination in the garden. The leaves, fresh or dried, have a bitter taste and add a bit of bite to salads and soups.

PICK YOUR POT

Hyssop grows well in medium traditional or self-watering containers. It's not a brute, and is happy to share space with other plants of similar size.

GROW IT

Start hyssop indoors about eight weeks before the last frost, or direct-sow in the spring. Pruning the growing tips and cutting the flowers for edible bouquets encourages the plant to become bushy and full. Hyssop prefers to grow in full sun, but does tolerate some shade.

EAT IT

Leaves and flowers can be harvested as needed and used to season salads, soups, and stews or dried for seasoning winter meals. Hyssop is best if harvested before its flowers bloom.

BUG OFF

Pests and diseases do not appear to be a problem.

PICK YOUR PLANT

'**Albus**': has white, rather than indigo, flowers

'**Sissinghurst**': has a more compact growth habit

Purple hyssop thrives in a self-watering strawberry planter.

LEMONGRASS

(*Cymbopogon citratus*)

*W*hat would you call something that looks like a clump of rather tall grass and smells of lemon? Lemongrass! This import from Southeast Asia is an essential ingredient in many Oriental dishes. Lemongrass is a good container plant and a decorative addition to a container garden.

Lemongrass is at home in a medium-size container.

PICK YOUR POT

Lemongrass likes water. If you're very diligent about watering, you can grow it in a traditional container, but it's easier to grow with less fussing in a small or medium self-watering container that is at least six inches deep.

GROW IT

Lemongrass has a tropical heritage; in addition to plenty of water, it likes rich soil, warmth, and sunlight. Give this plant a warm and sunny spot and a supplemental dose of liquid fertilizer every six weeks or so. Lemongrass can in theory be wintered over indoors, but its need for warmth and light makes that a laborious process. I treat it as an annual and buy new plants each year. Don't look for lemongrass seed — you won't find any (it's vegetatively propagated). You'll have to buy plants from your local nursery.

EAT IT

The culinary part of lemongrass is not the "grass," but rather the white heart at the base of mature stems. Pull the stems from the plant, trim the green part and any roots, and then peel the outer layers to expose the heart, which is sliced as an addition to stir-fries and soups.

BUG OFF

Pests and diseases do not appear to be a problem.

PICK YOUR PLANT

There are two species of lemongrass, only one of which, *Cymbopogon citratus,* is suitable for cooking. The other, *C. flexxuosis,* is grown for its oil, which is used in scented products like soaps, perfumes, and cleaners. Be sure you're getting the culinary lemongrass when you go to the nursery.

LEMON VERBENA

(*Aloysia triphylla*)

Lemon verbena lives up to its name: its lemon aroma wafts from the leaves when you brush against the plant, and the scent is even stronger if you crush the leaves. It's used to make a refreshing tea and can also be used sparingly in salads and stuffing.

PICK YOUR POT

Lemon verbena needs only moderate amounts of water; if the soil becomes sodden, the roots rot. I grow lemon verbena in a medium traditional container, and that seems to suit it.

GROW IT

Lemon verbena is usually propagated from cuttings, so it's best to buy the one plant you'll need from your local nursery. Lemon verbena likes a fertile soil and appreciates a supplemental feeding of liquid seaweed fertilizer every six weeks or so. Prune the plant regularly during the growing season to encourage bushy, compact growth.

This plant is used to a warm and sunny climate; give it as much sun you can. Don't plant lemon verbena outdoors until all danger of frost is past, and plan on bringing it inside before the first frost of autumn. Even when it is inside, lemon verbena will lose its leaves in the fall and go dormant for the winter. It's not dead, just resting. Water lightly, give it some sunlight, and make sure it doesn't freeze. It will revive in the spring.

EAT IT

Clip the leaves as you need them. The leaves are most fragrant when fresh, but they retain their scent well when dried.

BUG OFF

Unlike most other herbs, lemon verbena is bothered by pests, particularly whiteflies and spider mites. A row cover will prevent the insects from getting to the plant, but it's not a pretty solution. Insecticidal soap will kill the pests and is relatively nontoxic.

PICK YOUR PLANT

The straight species — *Aloysia triphylla* — is the plant usually found at nurseries and garden centers.

The foliage of lemon verbena retains its scent when dried.

MARJORAM

(*Origanum majorana*)

An oregano relative, marjoram finds its way into soups, stews, and myriad sauces. It comes from the Mediterranean, and therefore likes lots of sun and lean soil. To enhance its flavor, don't give it an easy ride. Marjoram is especially tasty when fresh, but can also be dried easily for winter use.

Marjoram gets just enough water in the pocket of a self-watering strawberry pot.

PICK YOUR POT

Plant your marjoram in a small-to-medium pot that's at least six inches deep. Either a traditional or self-watering container will suit marjoram.

GROW IT

Marjoram is frost sensitive and does not grow well in cold weather. Plant the tiny seeds indoors in late winter; just barely cover them with moist starting mix and continue to keep the soil moist. Germination is slow; it can take as long as two weeks. Transplant outdoors to a container after the last frost date. Because individual plants vary in taste, buying from a nursery has one advantage: you can smell-test the plants to find the ones that have the fragrance and taste you want.

EAT IT

Start harvesting tiny leaves any time after the plant is four inches tall and before flowers appear; either clip the individual leaves or cut whole stems and take off the leaves later. Keep the plant trimmed back to prevent flowering, which makes the leaves taste bitter. If you're drying marjoram, keep the leaves on the stems and remove them only when you want to use them. For the best flavor, add marjoram right at the end of the cooking process so the volatile oils don't dissipate.

BUG OFF

Pests and diseases do not appear to be a problem.

PICK YOUR PLANT

The straight species — *Origanum majorana* — is the only marjoram available.

MINT

(*Mentha* spp.)

We're really talking about a whole wonderful family of mints — spearmint, apple mint, chocolate mint. They're all different in taste, but they have similar needs. Prime among them? Solitude. Mints do not make good neighbors; they're aggressive and will take over any container they're in. The only fit companion for a mint is another mint.

PICK YOUR POT

Mint likes moderate and steady moisture, so it is a good candidate for a self-watering container. It will also do fine in a traditional container. If you grow different mints in the same container, try to pick ones with contrasting growth habits — place a low-growing one with a tall one. A small or medium container will grow all the mint you're likely to want.

GROW IT

You don't have to know how to grow mint: it grows itself. Mint takes a long time to grow from seed, so start with a small plant from the nursery, plant it, keep it watered, and let it be.

EAT IT

Pick the leaves whenever you want them; pruning the branch tips will encourage bushy growth. If you plan to dry the leaves, pick them before blossoms appear, for best flavor. Store dried mint leaves in an airtight jar.

BUG OFF

Pests and diseases do not appear to be a problem.

PICK YOUR PLANT

Apple mint: a hint of apple

Bergamot mint: a bit like breakfast tea

Chocolate mint: a chocolate-flavored spearmint

Ginger mint: has beautiful variegated leaves

Lavender mint: as the name implies . . .

Peppermint: you *know* what this tastes like

Pineapple mint: variegated leaves and a wonderful scent

Combining plants of different growth habits can yield a pleasing container combination. Here, apple mint (tall) complements variegated ginger mint (spreading).

OREGANO

(*Origanum* spp.)

Oregano's peppery and savory taste is part of almost every Greek and Italian dish — pasta sauce, pizza sauce, and anything with tomatoes, zucchini, or eggplant in it. Oregano is also a decorative plant with pretty flowers, which are also edible. The golden variety (pictured) adds a nice visual kick to any container combination.

Golden oregano adds a spot of color to the container garden.

PICK YOUR POT

Grow oregano in a medium traditional container in full sun. (In damp, rainy times, move oregano under cover to prevent overwatering.)

GROW IT

You can start oregano from seed, but it's not really a good idea. Oregano plants from the same batch of seed vary quite a bit in taste. Buy plants from a nursery after taste-testing to determine which ones you like most. Once you have an oregano you like, overwinter it in a cool place or propagate new plants from cuttings. Oregano is an easy keeper. It actually thrives on neglect, and responds badly to coddling: don't fertilize it; don't water it much. Just give it a place in the sun and water lightly.

EAT IT

Regular harvest of the leaves entices the plant to form a compact, bushy shape and stimulates leaf production. Leaves can be preserved by drying.

BUG OFF

Healthy oregano plants are rarely troubled by insect pests.

PICK YOUR PLANT

Golden oregano: attractive golden-hued leaf

Greek oregano: a good container choice; low-growing; stronger tasting than other varieties

'Herrenhausen': not as fragrant as the culinary oreganos but ornamental, with small purple blossoms

'Kent Beauty': pink flowers on a plant that is more ornamental than edible; suited to hanging baskets

PARSLEY

(*Petroselinum crispum*)

This carrot relative is a biennial (a plant that lives for two years, then sets seed and dies), but gardeners usually grow it as an annual. Although most often used as a garnish, parsley is a flavorful and healthful addition to salads, salad dressings, dips, and soups, not to mention an essential ingredient for most Italian dishes. It's also easy to grow.

PICK YOUR POT

Parsley does well in a self-watering container — it is quite happy with steady, moderate moisture. However, it's also content to grow in a traditional container. Whatever kind of container you choose should be at least eight inches deep.

GROW IT

In theory, you can direct-seed parsley outdoors in spring. In practice, parsley seeds take a very long time to germinate, as much as a month or even more. You can speed germination somewhat by soaking the seeds overnight or scalding them with boiling water before planting. Or you can let somebody else deal with the germination problem, and buy started plants from a nursery. Pick young, small plants that are deep green. Transplant parsley in the late spring; it's fairly hardy and can tolerate light frost.

EAT IT

Harvest the leaves, including the stems, whenever you want; the plant will replenish itself quickly.

BUG OFF

Pests and diseases do not appear to be a problem.

PICK YOUR PLANT

'Forest Green': a curly-leaf variety with long stems that help keep the leaves off the soil

Italian dark green: flat leaves and a fairly strong flavor

When planted in a self-watering hanging pot, 'Forest Green' parsley is easy to care for and to harvest.

ROSEMARY

(*Rosmarinus officinalis*)

Rosemary's distinctive fragrance adds a special something to tomato sauces, beans and squash, and roasted meats and poultry. It grows well with other plants, and has pretty blossoms that range from blue to pink and white. A woody plant of Mediterranean heritage, rosemary isn't hardy for us, but that just means we get to enjoy its company indoors through the winter.

Prostrate rosemary tastes just as good as the upright variety, but has a more casual, draping habit.

PICK YOUR POT

Rosemary tolerates dry soil, and generally does better in a traditional pot than in a self-watering container. Grow it in a medium traditional container that is at least eight inches deep. Alternatively, you can plant rosemary in one of the pockets of a strawberry pot, like the one shown in chapter two. Although the container is self-watering, the individual pockets do not appear to get enough moisture to trouble the plants. I've also grown rosemary successfully in a hanging self-watering container along with other herbs. I let the reservoir go dry periodically and water only when the soil is partially dry.

GROW IT

Rosemary is best propagated from root cuttings or by stem layering, neither of which I like to bother with. I purchase started plants at a nursery and transplant them to the container they'll spend the summer in. Rosemary is usually hardy to USDA Zone 7. We bring ours inside for the winter and give it a sunny window and occasional water.

PICK YOUR PLANT

You're likely to find named varieties at a nursery (especially if you live in a climate where rosemary grows year-round), but most have been selected for ornamental reasons — flower color (blue, pink, white) or plant habit (prostrate or upright) — rather than taste.

SAGE

(*Salvia officinalis*)

Sage is often grown for its good looks. Its soft, fragrant foilage comes in a range of colors from gray-green to dusky purple, and adds visual texture to a container planting. But sage is more than just a pretty face; it adds zest and a lemony boost to stuffing, stews, and omelets. It's also an essential part of any herbes de Provence *mix.*

PICK YOUR POT

Grow in either a traditional pot or a self-watering container.

GROW IT

Sage is best grown from cuttings, because it takes two years from seed to grow a productive plant. I buy plants from the nursery. Sage loves sun; grow it either alone or with plants that share its requirements.

EAT IT

Clip the leaves as soon as the plant is large enough to spare a few, making sure to take leaves from different places on the plant so it doesn't get lopsided. Sage is easy to dry; store it in an airtight container.

BUG OFF

Pests and diseases do not appear to be a problem.

PICK YOUR PLANT

'Holt's Mammoth': what's probably in your store-bought package of dried sage

'Purpurea': dusky purple, with a spreading growth habit

'Tricolor': green, cream, and pink/purple leaves

White sage: dusty gray-green foliage

If you're going to grow sage, why pick plain green? 'Purpurea' and 'Tricolor' jazz up any container combo.

SAVORY

(*Satureja* spp.)

There are two savory varieties used in cooking. Summer savory is the larger plant, at about a foot and a half tall. It has narrow, dark green leaves and a lavender flower, and is used in stuffing, rice, onion soup, and as a garnish for green beans. Winter savory is smaller, with very small green leaves and lilac flowers. Its stronger taste can be used as a pepper substitute and to flavor sauerkraut and dry beans.

Summer savory thrives with a traditional pot and lots of sun.

PICK YOUR POT

Savory is another member of the Mediterranean fraternity that wants sun and not much water; plant it in a small or medium traditional container that is about eight inches deep.

GROW IT

Savory can be direct-seeded after the last frost date or started indoors and transplanted. I grow only one plant, so I buy it from a nursery. Savory grows well in a traditional clay pot; let the soil dry out a bit between waterings.

EAT IT

Clip whole stems and remove the leaves afterward.

BUG OFF

Pests and disease do not appear to be a problem.

PICK YOUR PLANT

Summer savory (*Satureja hortenis*): see description above

Winter savory (*S. montana*): see description above

SHISO

(*Perilla frutescens*)

This is not your everyday green! A spicy edible ornamental from the Orient with a flavor of cinnamon and cloves, shiso has good looks and good taste. The young leaves are excellent in salads, and add an extra kick to stir-fries and casseroles. If for no other reason, grow shiso for its colorful foliage. Try combining all three varieties in a medium self-watering container.

PICK YOUR POT

Shiso likes water and does well in a self-watering container, either alone or with other plants of similar mature size (18 to 24 inches).

GROW IT

Shiso can be grown from seed, but it is a long and tricky process. I grow only one plant of any variety, so I purchase started plants at a nursery. Shiso is frost sensitive; delay transplanting it outdoors until after the last frost date.

EAT IT

Clip the leaves as soon as the plant is large enough that it won't miss them.

BUG OFF

Pests and diseases do not appear to be a problem.

PICK YOUR PLANT

Britton shiso: foliage is green on top and red underneath

Green shiso: green foliage

Red shiso: red foliage

The spicy foilage of red shiso makes a bold addition to container compositions.

TARRAGON

(*Artemisia dracunculus* var. *sativa*)

I'm not sure how to describe the taste of tarragon. Is it like basil? Licorice? Fennel? Or all of the above? This herb gives a special flavor to baked fish and poultry (you can't make chicken tarragon without it!), and it makes a wonderful vinegar. The silvery foliage of tarragon is especially attractive in container combinations.

Silvery French tarragon lends a taste of licorice to a variety of dishes.

PICK YOUR POT

Small, with a bushy habit, tarragon is a very good container plant. Use a small or medium traditional container that is about eight inches deep.

GROW IT

French tarragon, which is the best culinary variety, is grown from cuttings, not seeds. You'll need to buy plants already started at a nursery. Of Mediterranean heritage, tarragon thrives on lots of sun and warmth and not a lot of water. Give it a nice sunny spot, and let the soil dry between waterings.

EAT IT

Clip the top four to six inches of the stems to stimulate new growth and a bushy shape. Tarragon's volatile oils dissipate if it is cooked too long, so add it late in the cooking process.

BUG OFF

Pests and diseases do not appear to be a problem.

PICK YOUR PLANT

Make sure you're getting French tarragon (*A. d.* var. *sativa*); Russian tarragon (*A. d.* var. *inodora*) is bitter and barely edible. Another alternative is not technically a tarragon at all — Mexican tarragon tastes like French tarragon, but is actually a marigold (*Tagetes lucida*). It has small, deep yellow flowers and edible foliage.

THYME

(*Thymus* spp.)

Thyme comes in many, many shapes and various flavors, all with characteristic tiny leaves and adorned with little flowers that may be lavender, mauve, pink, or white. Thyme's flavor is strongest when the leaves are fresh or recently dried. Thyme blossoms do a great job of attracting bees and other pollinators to the garden.

PICK YOUR POT

Thyme is another member of the Mediterranean fraternity that is used to the sort of hot and dry climate that would kill off most other garden plants. It does best with intermittent access to water, and should be grown in a small traditional container about six inches deep.

GROW IT

I would much rather try one each of many different thymes than have many of any one. Therefore, I don't bother starting plants from seed; I buy from a nursery, where I can sniff and taste the possibilities. Don't fuss over your thyme; don't fertilize it and don't water it too often. Just harvest the leaves whenever you want and bring the pot inside for the winter so you can have fresh thyme all year long.

EAT IT

Once the plant is established and growing, you can harvest the leaves whenever you like. Cut off about a third of the stem, taking your cuttings at different places to give the plant a full and even shape.

PICK YOUR PLANT

There are dozens of different thymes. Here are just few to start you off:

Creeping thyme: will drape nicely over the side of a hanging container; has lavender flowers

Orange thyme: sweet with a hint of citrus

Summer thyme: compact with a pungent, spicy flavor

Summer thyme thrives in the pocket of a self-watering strawberry planter.

CHAPTER FOURTEEN

The EDIBLE BOUQUET

What would a garden be without flowers? Well, if I'm going to plant flowers in my container garden, I want to be able to eat them! Edible flowers add a spot of color and spice to the menu, in addition to dressing up the deck. And, like their brothers and sisters of the vegetable world, edible flowers thrive in self-watering containers.

BACHELOR'S BUTTON

(Centaurea cyanus)

Also known as cornflower, and sometimes listed in catalogs under its botanical name, bachelor's button flowers are often used as a garnish in salads and desserts. Although best known for its deep blue flowers, it also comes in red, pink, and white. Butterflies and pollinating insects are attracted to them.

When deadheaded regularly, bachelor's button will bloom through the summer.

PICK YOUR POT

Bachelor's button will grow well in either a traditional or self-watering container.

GROW IT

Bachelor's button can be direct-sown in late spring or early summer, or started indoors and transplanted. Seedlings of bachelor's button are also available at most garden centers and nurseries. This plant is an easy keeper; just keep it watered.

EAT IT

Pick the flowers just after they have opened and spinkle the petals in salads. Deadhead regularly to keep the plant producing.

BUG OFF

Pests and diseases do not appear to be a problem.

PICK YOUR PLANT

'**Black Gem**' or '**Garnet**': ruffled dark maroon

'**Blue Boy**': the classic cornflower blue

Choice mix: a mixture of blue, pink, red, and white

Frosty mix: bicolored; dark centers of maroon and purple with white outer petals

'**Red Boy**': a dark red heirloom variety introduced in 1941

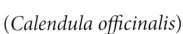

CALENDULA

(*Calendula officinalis*)

This large, daisylike flower adds a boost of color to any container combination. It also provides tasty petals for a garnish in salads or with cooked vegetables. Calendulas also make excellent cut flowers for the dinner table; a cheerful bouquet of yellow and orange blooms can last as long as five days in a vase of fresh water.

PICK YOUR POT

Calendulas can be grown in medium-size traditional or self-watering containers.

GROW IT

Start calendulas indoors in early spring and transplant when the plants are about two inches tall, or purchase young plants from a nursery. Just put them in a sunny place and keep them watered. Harvest the flowers regularly and deadhead any that are past their prime in order to keep the plant producing new blooms. Calendula plants will bloom over a long season.

EAT IT

Cut the flowers with some stem to hang on to. Remove the petals and sprinkle them over whatever you're serving.

BUG OFF

Pests and diseases do not appear to be a problem.

PICK YOUR PLANT

'Bon Bon': orange, yellow, and apricot with double flowers

'Lemon Beauty': double yellow flowers

Pacific Beauty mix: apricot, pale yellow, deep orange

'Red Heart': maroon centers with petals that are maroon on the back and orange on the front

'Sunshine Flashback': petals are orange on top and red on the underside

Yellow calendula is a great container partner for pink dianthus and golden oregano.

The lush, orange blooms of Pacific Beauty mix calendulas fill a medium self-watering container.

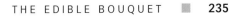

DIANTHUS

(*Dianthus barbatus*)

*S*ometimes known as sweet William, sometimes as "pinks" (though they come in many other colors too), dianthus provides colorful and spicy petals as a garnish for fruit salads and baked desserts. Their scent and taste are somewhat clovelike. Because the plants stay compact, they're easily tucked in with other container plants for a shot of color.

The pink blooms of dianthus, planted in a traditional glazed pot, stand out against the green background of the garden.

PICK YOUR POT

Dianthus will grow well in either traditional or self-watering containers, with or without neighbors.

GROW IT

Start seeds indoors three to four weeks before the last frost date and transplant seedlings to containers when there are several sets of true leaves. I buy plants from a nursery so I can get a few plants with a variety of colors. Sweet William likes full sun but does not like very hot weather; at the end of a very hot day, give it a bit of shade. Keep the flowers picked, and deadhead any that are past their prime.

EAT IT

Harvest by clipping the flower stems with pruners or floral scissors. The white part at the base of the petals is bitter; remove it by grasping the petals with one hand and clipping off the base of the flower.

BUG OFF

Doesn't appear to be significantly affected by pests or disease.

PICK YOUR PLANT

There are many. Pick the ones whose colors appeal to you. Some of my favorites are in the Amazon Neon series: 'Amazon Neon Purple', 'Amazon Neon Cherry', and 'Amazon Neon Rose Magic'.

MARIGOLD

(*Tagetes tenuifolia*)

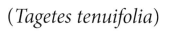

Not all marigolds are meant to be eaten. The ones you want in your dinner are called gem marigolds or signet marigolds. The other varieties aren't poisonous, but they don't taste good. Marigold petals add color and spice to salads and cooked vegetables. They also attract butterflies, which is reason enough to grow them even if you don't eat them.

PICK YOUR POT

Plant in a medium-size traditional container where they can dry out periodically; they get too much water in self-watering containers and will rot.

GROW IT

Start marigold seeds three or four weeks before the last frost date and transplant to containers after the danger of frost is past, or direct-sow after the last frost date. My local nursery offers gem marigolds, so I buy them there. Marigolds pretty much take care of themselves; just give them a place in the sun and clip any dead blossoms. That's all there is to it.

EAT IT

Clip the flowers as needed. Remove the bitter white part at the base of the petals before eating.

BUG OFF

Pests and diseases don't appear to be a problem.

PICK YOUR PLANT

Make sure you're getting marigolds from the gem series. They are named for the color they bear: 'Lemon Gem', 'Tangerine Gem', and 'Golden Gem'.

'Lemon Gem' marigolds bloom prolifically in an ordinary terra-cotta pot.

NASTURTIUM

(*Tropaeolum majus*)

Here's the diva of the edible flower opera. This one's not just for looks; the large petals have a distinctive peppery taste that adds flavor as well as color to potato salad, egg salad, pasta salads, and cold soups. And that's only half the story: the leaves are edible too, with a spicy tang reminiscent of watercress. They're an attractive addition to any salad.

We plant Jewel mix nasturtiums in traditional pots to keep them from growing out of control.

PICK YOUR POT

In a self-watering container filled with a compost-based soil, this plant goes on a botanical binge; it grows bigger, makes more flowers and leaves, and crowds out anything else growing in the container. If you'd rather that didn't happen, grow nasturtiums in a traditional container and don't be too fussy about watering every time the soil dries out a bit.

GROW IT

Nasturtiums do not transplant well; direct-sow the seeds in a container after the danger of frost is past. Nasturtiums are hardy folk, able to grow even in fairly poor soil and to survive some stretches of very little water. That's not to say, however, that they really like living on the edge, the way some herbs do. Given a rich soil and as much water as they want, nasturtiums go wild.

EAT IT

Pick flowers whenever you need them; they will be quickly replaced. Leaves are best when harvested at silver-dollar size.

BUG OFF

Aphids consider nasturtium an edible plant, too. In hot weather, check the undersides of the leaves for these pests. See chapter nine for ways to deal with aphids, or simply remove badly infested leaves and drop them in a can of soapy water.

PICK YOUR PLANT

Nasturtiums come in two versions. The standard one is a fairly compact, bushy plant. The alternate is a vine that can, depending on how you train it, either climb a trellis or wander the neighborhood. The latter is identified in catalogs as trailing nasturtium. Varieties differ by color, which can range from cream through pink and yellow to orange and red. I enjoy being a bit adventurous, so I lean toward mixes of different colors:

'Brilliant': crimson flowers

Jewel mix: combines single and double blooms in red, pink, orange, salmon, and cherry

'Moongleam': double soft yellow flowers

'Tip Top Apricot': apricot blooms on a compact plant

Trailing nasturium mix: red, rose, orange, and yellow that will drape over the side of a hanging container

Jewel mix nasturtiums come in a range of color combinations.

THE INCREDIBLE, EDIBLE NASTURTIUM

Rarely will you come across such a beautiful plant that can be eaten in so many ways. Like any other edible flower, the fragrant blossoms of nasturtium can be added to salads or used as a garnish. That's easy enough. They also make a tasty appetizer when stuffed with cream cheese (this is also a good way to eat squash blossoms, by the way). Most vegetable gardeners know that the leaves are a special, spicy addition to mesclun mixes, especially when harvested on the small side (silver-dollar size).

But wait! There's more. The seeds are edible, too, and when pickled can be used as a substitute for capers. Don't rush out and start opening seed packets for dinner, though. What you're after are fresh, green nasturtium seeds, harvested right from the plant. Wait until the blooms have faded, then harvest the fruit that remains behind. The fruit is made up of three compartments, each of which contains a seed; separate the compartments as you harvest them.

To pickle the seeds, bring them to a boil in vinegar with salt, peppercorns, and a bay leaf, then store them (after cooling) in a clean jar in the refrigerator. Use the pickled seeds in recipes that call for capers.

SUNFLOWER

(*Helianthus annuus*)

Sunflowers come in a range of sizes, but it is the dwarfs that make good container plants. Different dwarf varieties grow to different heights, but they all stay between eight inches and two feet. The immature buds are edible, steamed or sautéed. If you eat the buds, though, you don't get the flowers, the petals of which add a tangy taste to salads, soups, and cooked summer vegetables. If you eat the flowers, you don't get the seeds, which are a well-known and well-liked snack.

I usually forgo the seed treat at the end of the harvest, to attract birds to the garden. Like many other flowers, edible and otherwise, sunflowers also attract bees.

PICK YOUR POT

Sunflowers grow well in self-watering containers and benefit from the fertility of a compost-based mix. I've found that dwarf sunflowers are content to share a medium container with other edible flowers.

GROW IT

Unless you have a fairly long growing season, start sunflowers indoors two or three weeks before the last frost date and transplant to containers after the danger of frost is past. Nurseries often have sunflower plants, but make sure you're getting a dwarf variety; full-size sunflowers are not container plants.

EAT IT

Harvest buds before the flowers start to open. Harvest petals by pulling them from the flowers. If you don't want to share the seeds with birds and squirrels, cover the flowers with paper bags until the seeds are plump and move a bit when you wiggle them. (I'll admit to skipping that step and leaving some seeds for the birds — I can buy more sunflower seeds, but I can't buy chickadees for my container garden.)

BUG OFF

Unless you call chickadees pests, I haven't had any problems.

PICK YOUR PLANT

'Bashful': pale yellow flowers with pink toward the center

'Big Smile': an early-blooming extra-dwarf variety with three- to six-inch blooms; perfect for containers

'Firecracker': many red and gold flowers

VIOLAS

(*Viola* spp.)

*V*iola is a catchall name for a whole bunch of related flowers: pansies, violas (sometimes called horned violet or tufted pansy), and violets, including the ubiquitous Johnny-jump-up. There's not a flower in the garden, edible or not, that is more likely to put a smile on my face; they're the bluebirds of flowers. We often add them to a bowl of lettuce to turn a salad into a celebration.

PICK YOUR POT

Violas grow well in either self-watering containers or traditional pots, and they share space willingly with other plants.

GROW IT

There really isn't much you have to know about growing vio-
littleJohnny-jump-ups, will scat-

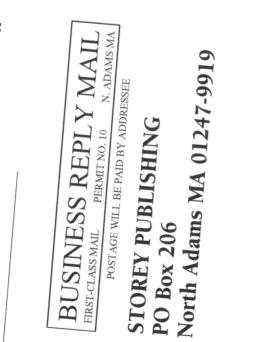

NO POSTAGE
NECESSARY
IF MAILED
IN THE
UNITED STATES

BUSINESS REPLY MAIL
FIRST-CLASS MAIL   PERMIT NO. 10   N. ADAMS MA

POSTAGE WILL BE PAID BY ADDRESSEE

STOREY PUBLISHING
PO Box 206
North Adams MA 01247-9919

From:

la-
he

'Jolly Joker' violas fare well in a traditional terra-cotta pot.

Acknowledgments

I have been fortunate in that many of the people who helped me with *The Vegetable Gardener's Bible* also helped me with this book, though this time around they had different parts in the play.

Gwen Steege acted in the role of acquisitions editor this time and helped to mature a "good idea" into a proposal for a book. Maggie Lydic helped me to move from a general proposal to an outline and a fuller understanding of what needed to go into this book. Giles Prett, now an avid gardener, hadn't done garden photography since his work on *The Vegetable Gardener's Bible*. He came out of "retirement" to help us with this book.

Cindy McFarland, art director, had a vision for this book and helped all of us to share that vision and bring together words and images. Jessica Armstrong was responsible for designing and building the pages of this book, from an assemblage of more than 70,000 words and 3,600 images.

Carleen Perkins, my editor, gave me continual support and feedback as I chose the seemingly endless words it took to communicate my vision of a different way to garden. This book is better than it would have been because I had Carleen's patient help along the way.

Nathaniel Smith shouldered an extra share of the homestead work so that Sylvia and I would have time for The Book. Gardener's Supply Company provided us with numerous self-watering containers and other gardening tools and supplies. Without their help, I could not have conducted the extensive trials upon which this book is based. Earth Box supplied me with its self-watering containers for testing. Peaceful Valley Farm and Garden Supply sent me garden tools and supplies. Vermont Compost Company supplied compost and compost-based container mixes.

Photography Credits

Courtesy of All-America Selections: 79, 155

© **David Cavagnaro:** 149 middle; 178; 228 bottom

Courtesy of Gardener's Supply Company: 139 all except 2nd from top

© **MACORE, Inc.:** 163 middle

© **Giles Prett/Fotografix:** 2; 3 left; 5; 6-7; 11; 12; 13; 15; 16 top, middle; 21 bottom; 23 right; 24 right; 25 left, center; 28; 31; 32; 34; 35; 36; 37; 38; 39; 40; 43 top; 45; 46; 47 bottom; 48; 49; 50; 52 top left, bottom left; 53; 55 top, second from top; 56; 57; 58; 65; 66; 67; 68; 70; 71; 73 except bottom right; 74-75; 77; 78 top left; 81 bottom; 82; 83; 84; 85; 86; 88; 89; 90; 91; 92; 93; 94; 98 left; 99 right; 101; 104; 112; 113 all except bottom center and bottom right; 116; 117; 119; 120 top right; 126 top right; 132; 137 bottom right; 138; 142 top; 143 top, middle; 144 bottom; 147 middle; 150; 152 bottom; 153 bottom; 154 bottom; 156 bottom; 158 bottom; 159 bottom; 161 top; 164 bottom; 166 top, middle; 172; 173; 174 top, middle; 182; 189 right; 196 top; 197 top, middle; 202 bottom left; 204 bottom; 207 bottom right; 213 top; 217 bottom; 220; 223 bottom; 225 bottom; 227 middle; 234-235 bottom; 240 bottom; 242-243; 246; 247

Nathaniel E. Smith: 80

Sylvia Ferry Smith: 9 right (all); 16 bottom; 17; 19; 21 top; 22; 22-23 bottom; 24 left, center; 25 right; 26; 27; 29; 33; 44-45; 47 top, middle; 52 middle left, right; 55 second from bottom, bottom; 59 right; 63; 64-65; 69; 72 top; 73 bottom right; 76; 78 all except top left; 81 top; 87; 95; 96; 100 left; 102-103; 106; 107; 108-109 bottom; 110; 113 bottom center, bottom right; 114 top; 118-119; 120 all except top right; 121; 122; 123; 124; 125 left (all); 126 all except top right; 128-129; 130 left; 131; 133 top; 134; 135; 136-137; 137 all except bottom right; 140-141; 142 bottom; 144 top; 145; 146; 147 top, bottom right; 148; 149 top; 151 top, middle; 152 top; 153 middle; 154 top; 155 top, middle; 156 middle; 157 middle; 160 middle; 161 bottom; 162; 164 top; 165; 167; 168; 169 top, middle; 170 middle; 171; 175; 176; 177; 179; 180; 181 top, middle; 183 middle; 184; 185 top, middle; 186 top, middle; 187 top, middle, bottom right; 188 top, middle; 189 top; 190 top, middle; 191 middle; 192; 193 top, middle; 194; 195 top, middle; 196 bottom; 198; 199; 200; 201; 202 top; 203 top, middle; 204 top; 205; 206 top, middle; 207 top; 210; 211 top, middle; 212; 215; 216; 217 top, middle; 218 top; 219; 221 top; 222; 223 top, middle; 224; 225 top, middle; 226; 227 top; 228 top; 229; 230; 231; 234; 235 top, bottom right; 236; 237; 238; 239; 240 top; 241

© **Storey Publishing, LLC:** 51; 69 bottom; 72 bottom; 100 bottom; 115; 139 second from top; 174 right

© **Martin Wall:** 149 bottom right; 213; 214; 221

© **Jim Westphalen/Westphalen Photography:** 8-9; 10-11; 18-19; 30-31; 54-55; 61; 97; 208-209; 232-233; 235 middle

© **Lee Ann White/Positive Images:** 218 bottom

Further Reading

The Bountiful Container
Rose Marie Nichols McGee and Maggie Stuckey, Workman Publishing, 2002
This is the book that brought vegetable gardening in containers out of the closet. Very thorough, solid information about how to grow many edibles in traditional, hole-in-the-bottom containers. It's also a fun read, full of historical asides and little-known facts.

The Gardener's A–Z Guide to Growing Organic Food
Tanya L.K. Denckla, Storey Publishing, 2003
Whether you garden in the earth or in containers, this book belongs on your shelf. It is full of information about all aspects of gardening. When do you plant? When do you harvest? What bug is that eating my cabbage, and what can I do about it? All that and lots more, well organized, clearly written.

Four-Season Harvest
Eliot Coleman, Chelsea Green Publishing, 1992
Although it's about gardening in the earth, with an emphasis on season extension, this book is a good resource for gardeners regardless of where they live. A gardening classic.

Suppliers

Baker Creek Heirloom Seeds
2278 Baker Creek Road
Mansfield, MO 65704
Phone: (417) 924-8917
Fax: (417) 924-8887
www.RareSeeds.com

Heirloom, open-pollinated seeds; books.

Burpee Seeds and Plants
300 Park Avenue
Warminster, PA 18974-0565
Phone: (800) 888-1447
Fax: (800) 487-5530
www.burpee.com

Seeds, plants, and gardening supplies.

The Cook's Garden
P. O. Box C5030
Warminster, PA 18974
Phone: (800) 457-9703
Fax: (800) 457-9705
www.cooksgarden.com

Seeds, plants, gardening supplies, and books.

Earth Box
P. O. Box 420
St. Petersburg, FL 33731
Phone: (888) 917-3908
www.earthbox.com

Self-watering containers.

Fedco Seeds
P. O. Box 520
Waterville, ME 04903-0520
Phone: (207) 873-7333
Fax: (207) 872-8317
www.fedcoseeds.com

Seeds, seed potatoes, gardening supplies, and books.

Gardener's Supply Company
128 Intervale Road
Burlington, VT 05401-2850
Phone: (800) 876-5520
Fax: (800) 551-6712
www.gardeners.com

Extensive selection of self-watering and other containers, container mixes, gardening supplies.

Gardens Alive!
5100 Schenley Place
Lawrenceburg, IN 47025
Phone: (513) 354-1482
www.GardensAlive.com

Organic gardening supplies.

Harris Seeds
P. O. Box 24966
Rochester, NY 14692-0966
Phone: (800) 514-4441
Fax: (877) 892-9197
www.harrisseeds.com

Seeds, gardening supplies.

Johnny's Selected Seeds
955 Benton Avenue
Winslow, ME 04901-2601
Phone: (800) 879-2258
Fax: (800) 738-6314
www.Johnnyseeds.com

Seeds, plants, gardening supplies, self-watering containers, books. An excellent catalog full of information about growing, including recommended varieties for containers.

Nichols Garden Nursery
1190 Old Salem Road NE
Albany, OR 97321-4580
Phone: (800) 422-3985
Fax: (800) 231-5306
www.nicholsgardennursery.com

Seeds, plants, gardening supplies, and books.

Peaceful Valley Farm Supply
P.O. Box 2209
125 Clydesdale Court
Grass Valley, CA 95945
Phone: (888) 784-1722
Fax: (530) 272-4794
www.groworganic.com

This catalog has everything: seeds, gardening supplies, books, fertilizers, and soil amendments. Most important, this catalog tells you how to use what the company sells. The information is first-rate. Belongs on the shelf along with your best gardening books.

Pinetree Garden Seeds
P.O. Box 300
New Gloucester, ME 04260
Phone: (207) 926-3400
Fax: (888) 527-3337
www.superseeds.com

Seeds, gardening supplies, and books.

Vermont Compost Company
1996 Main Street
Montpelier, VT 05602
Phone: (802) 223-6049
Fax: (802) 223-9028
www.vermontcompost.com

Compost and compost-based container mixes.

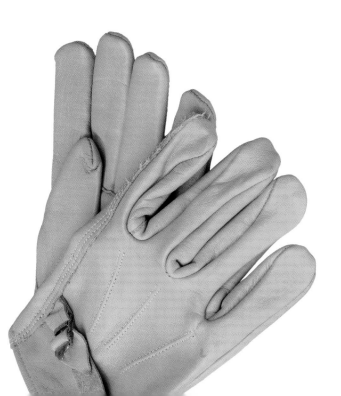

USDA Hardiness Zone Map

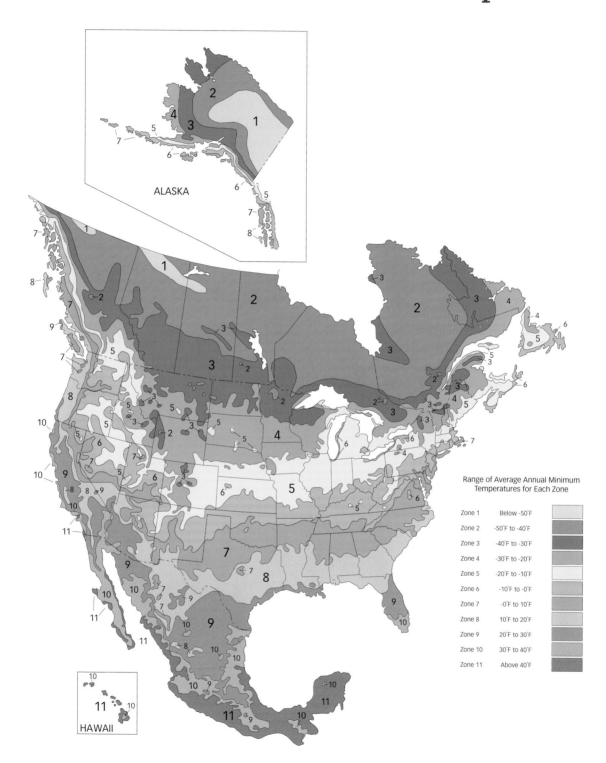

ALASKA

HAWAII

Range of Average Annual Minimum Temperatures for Each Zone

Zone 1	Below -50˚F
Zone 2	-50˚F to -40˚F
Zone 3	-40˚F to -30˚F
Zone 4	-30˚F to -20˚F
Zone 5	-20˚F to -10˚F
Zone 6	-10˚F to -0˚F
Zone 7	-0˚F to 10˚F
Zone 8	10˚F to 20˚F
Zone 9	20˚F to 30˚F
Zone 10	30˚F to 40˚F
Zone 11	Above 40˚F

Average Last Frost Dates: *United States and Canada*

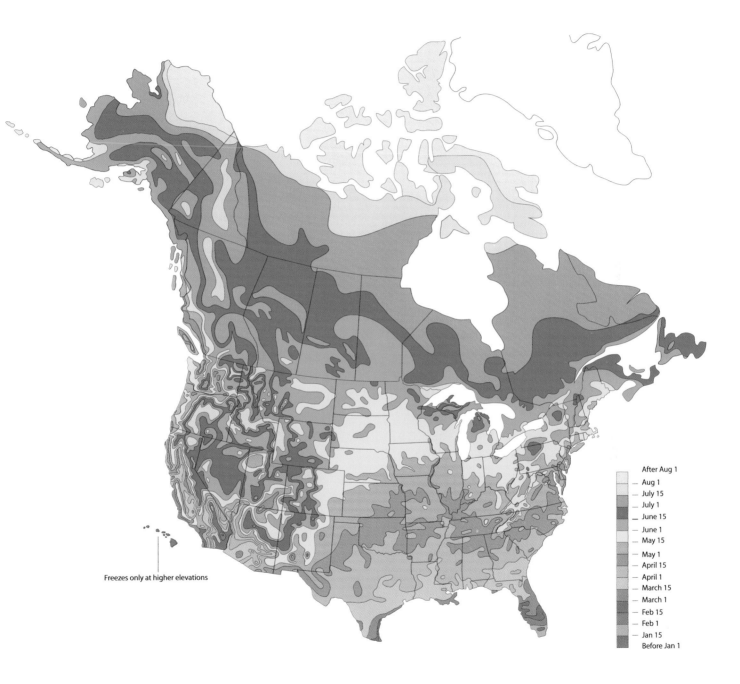

Freezes only at higher elevations

After Aug 1
— Aug 1
— July 15
— July 1
— June 15
— June 1
— May 15
— May 1
— April 15
— April 1
— March 15
— March 1
— Feb 15
— Feb 1
— Jan 15
Before Jan 1

Index

Page numbers in *italics* indicate illustrations. Page numbers in **bold** indicate tables.

Other Storey Titles You Will Enjoy

The Vegetable Gardener's Bible, by Edward C. Smith

By integrating four principles – Wide rows, Organic methods, Raised beds, and Deep soil – Smith reinvents vegetable gardening, showing everyone how to have their most successful garden ever. 320 pages. Paperback. ISBN 1-58017-212-1.

The Garden-Fresh Vegetable Cookbook, by Andrea Chesman

Take advantage of each season's freshest flavors with 275 recipes developed to help home cooks bring out the best in garden-fresh vegetables, with 14 master recipes that can accommodate whatever happens to be in your produce basket. 512 pages. Jacketed hardcover. ISBN 1-58017-534-1.

The Gardener's A-Z Guide to Growing Organic Food, by Tanya L.K. Denckla

This invaluable resource for organic gardeners provides in-depth growing, harvesting, and storing information for 765 varieties of vegetables, fruits, herbs, and nuts. For a healthy crop, organic remedies for 201 garden pests and diseases are included. 496 pages. Paperback. ISBN 1-58017-370-5.

The Classic Zucchini Cookbook,
by Nancy C. Ralston, Marynor Jordan, and Andrea Chesman

This completely revised and updated edition contains 225 through-the-menu recipes; an illustrated zucchini and squash primer; and information on how to select, store, clean, preserve, and substitute. 320 pages. Paperback. ISBN 1-58017-453-1.

The Tomato Festival Cookbook, by Lawrence Davis-Hollander

For the millions of people who love warm, lush, juicy, vine-ripened tomatoes, here is a stunning collection of 150 recipes that highlight glorious summer tomatoes as well as history; folklore; and growing, preserving, and seed-saving advice. 320 pages. Paperback. ISBN 1-58017-498-1.

The Garden-Fresh Vegetable Cookbook, by Andrea Chesman

Take advantage of each season's freshest flavors with 275 recipes developed to help home cooks bring out the best in garden-fresh vegetables, with 14 master recipes that can accommodate whatever happens to be in your produce basket. 512 pages. Jacketed hardcover. ISBN 1-58017-534-1.

The Big Book of Preserving the Harvest, by Carol W. Costenbader

Now even the busiest folks can create a well-stocked pantry of fruits, vegetables, flavored vinegars, pickles, chutneys, and seasonings. This indispensable kitchen reference for cooks of all levels will help anyone handle and manage produce fresh from the market or garden. 352 pages. Paperback. ISBN 1-58017-458-2.

These books and other Storey books are available wherever books are sold
and directly from Storey Publishing, 210 MASS MoCA Way, North Adams, MA 01247,
or by calling 1-800-441-5700. www.storey.com